Macromedia®

Dreamweaver® MX 2004
KillerTips

The hottest collection of cool tips and hidden secrets for Dreamweaver

Joseph Lowery
Angela C. Buraglia

Killer Tips series developed by Scott Kelby

PUBLISHER
Stephanie Wall

PRODUCTION MANAGER
Gina Kanouse

SENIOR ACQUISITIONS EDITOR
Linda Anne Bump

COPY EDITOR
Keith Cline

INDEXER
Lisa Stumpf

COMPOSITION
Amy Hassos

MANUFACTURING COORDINATOR
Dan Uhrig

COVER DESIGN AND CREATIVE CONCEPTS
Felix Nelson

MARKETING
Scott Cowlin
Tammy Detrich
Hannah Onstad Latham

PUBLICITY MANAGER
Susan Nixon

www.newriders.com
www.dwkillertips.com

International Standard Book Number: 0-7357-1379-0

Library of Congress Catalog Card Number: 2003111990

Printed in the United States of America

First printing: November, 2003

08 07 06 05 04   7 6 5 4 3 2

Interpretation of the printing code: The rightmost double-digit number is the year of the book's printing; the rightmost single-digit number is the number of the book's printing. For example, the printing code 03-1 shows that the first printing of the book occurred in 2003.

Trademarks

All terms mentioned in this book that are known to be trademarks or service marks have been appropriately capitalized. New Riders Publishing cannot attest to the accuracy of this information. Use of a term in this book should not be regarded as affecting the validity of any trademark or service mark.

Warning and Disclaimer

Every effort has been made to make this book as complete and as accurate as possible, but no warranty of fitness is implied. The information is provided on an as-is basis. The authors and New Riders Publishing shall have neither liability nor responsibility to any person or entity with respect to any loss or damages arising from the information contained in this book or from the use of the CD or programs that may accompany it.

ACKNOWLEDGMENTS

A special tip o' the hat to the hardest-working team in the Killer Tips biz: Derren, Jay, and especially Angela. We've had a great time gathering these tips—of course, I also enjoy running in front of a steamroller— and it's been a blast working together. I really appreciate the seriously hard effort put into the work by all concerned. Thanks also to the folks at New Riders: Linda, Gina, Keith, Lisa, Amy, and all the rest. And, of course, we wouldn't be anywhere without the Dreamweaver team—special thanks for developing a killer product.

—*JOSEPH LOWERY*

· ·

Thanks to my co-author, Joseph Lowery, who is an incredible inspiration not only to me, but also to many Dreamweaver fans worldwide. His sense of humor and ability to stay positive through stressful times has been a very positive influence on me. I also want to thank Matt Brown, Jay A. Grantham, and Derren Whiteman for their watchful tech-editing eyes. A bonus thanks goes to Jay for helping with screenshots again this time around. They really pulled through for us and got the job done. It is always a pleasure working with the New Riders team: Linda, Gina, Keith, Amy, and Lisa.

Very special thanks to Daniel Short for endless help and support. (I owe you "one or three," Dan.) I truly appreciate the ideas for tips you've sent me Massimo. To my friends who've supported me along the way, thank you.

Mom and Dad, if it weren't for your constant help and support, I don't know what I'd do or where I'd be. Thank you for everything.

—*ANGELA C. BURAGLIA*

ABOUT THE AUTHORS

Joseph Lowery is the author of *Joseph Lowery's Beyond Dreamweaver* and the co-author of a forthcoming book titled *Macromedia Dreamweaver MX 2004 Web Application Recipes* (New Riders) as well as the *Dreamweaver MX Bible* and the *Fireworks MX Bible* (both John Wiley & Sons). His books are international best-sellers, having sold more than 300,000 copies worldwide in 9 different languages. As a programmer, Joseph contributed two extensions to the latest release of Fireworks MX. He also is a consultant and trainer and has presented at Seybold in both Boston and San Francisco, Macromedia UCON in the United States and Europe, ThunderLizard's Web World, and other locations around the globe—ranging from New Zealand to Las Vegas. In partnership with Edoardo Zubler, Joseph developed FlashBang!—Flash navigation for Dreamweaver users.

. . . .

Angela C. Buraglia used to be a makeup artist for independent film, but she needed a career that would allow her to work from home and raise her son. Although she intended only to be a web developer, life's path has led her to become that and more. She is perhaps best known as the founder of DreamweaverFAQ.com, a site dedicated to serving the Dreamweaver community and which she continues to run today with Daniel Short. In addition to this book, she is a co-author of *Dreamweaver MX 2004 Magic* and contributing author to the previous edition (New Riders), the lead technical editor for the *Dreamweaver MX Bible* (John Wiley & Sons) and contributing author to *ColdFusion MX Web Application Construction Kit* (Macromedia Press).

Angela's future plans are to continue developing DreamweaverFAQ.com, to build and sell Dreamweaver extensions, to give presentations at conferences, and to continue with her involvement in Cartweaver. Long gone are the days of applying makeup; now Angela applies behaviors and CSS to websites and—most importantly—is home with her little boy.

These contributors devoted their considerable hands-on expertise to the entire development process for *Dreamweaver MX 2004 Killer Tips*. As this book was being written, these dedicated professionals reviewed all the material for technical content, organization, and flow. Their feedback was critical to ensuring that *Dreamweaver MX 2004 Killer Tips* fits our reader's need for the highest-quality technical information.

Jay A. Grantham is the owner, developer, chief cook, and bottle washer of WebsiteIC web development. He is a contributing author to the Dreamweaver reference site dwfaq.com, a member of the International Webmasters Association, and has done peer reviews for many authors. He enjoys learning what Dreamweaver can do for him and what he can do for the Dreamweaver community. Jay lives in Houston with is wife/best friend, Dana, and their two small children, Garrett and Katelyn. When he is not online, he is most likely fighting fires and saving lives as a member of the Houston Fire Department.

Derren Whiteman began building web sites by hand and later took up Dreamweaver after joining Mediafear, a San Francisco web design shop where he spent 3 years building web sites. Derren has also served as an information technology consultant and computer instructor. He spends much of his time in technical publishing. He cowrote the *Fireworks MX Bible* (John Wiley & Sons), served as technical editor for versions 3 and 4 of the *Fireworks Bible* and all versions of the *Dreamweaver Bible* (John Wiley & Sons) beginning with version 4, and has numerous other titles under his belt. Derren is a Macromedia Certified Dreamweaver Developer and maintains a number of web sites, including FrancinePaul.com, Konis.com, and Derren.com. He makes his home in Toronto.

Matt Brown is a consultant based in the Bay Area. He has edited more than 20 Dreamweaver and Photoshop books over the years. He has taught at Foothill College and the Multimedia Studies Program at San Francisco State University. He was on the Dreamweaver team for 5 years in a number of capacities, finally as Community Manager. Matt is married to a magnificent woman, Marcella, and keeps chickens and loves to cook and create all sorts of art.

Dan Short is the Chief Developer for Web Shorts Site Design as well as a devoted Team Macromedia Volunteer and uses almost the entire Macromedia Studio including Fireworks, ColdFusion, and Dreamweaver. He helps to maintain several HTML and Dreaweaver reference sites including www.dwfaq.com, for which he created the style changer and all ASP functionality, including the Snippets Exchange and the DWfaq Store. Dan is the co-author of Dreamweaver MX 2004 Magic, and contributing author of the previous edition. He's also written articles for several resource sites, including AListApart.com, Spider-Food.net, the MM Designer and Developer Center (www.macromedia.com/desdev) and DWfaq.com. Dan is also a contributing author for the dynamic chapters in the *Dreamweaver MX 2004 Bible* (Wiley) and the previous edition. He has also presented at several Dreamweaver conferences including the first two TODCONs and MXNorth in March of 2003.

TABLE OF CONTENTS

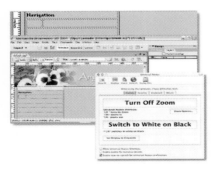

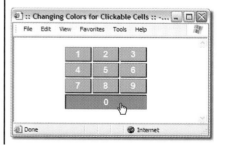

TABLE OF CONTENTS

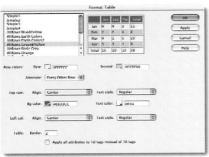

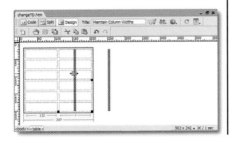

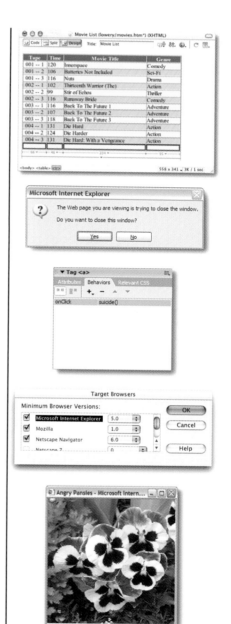

TABLE OF CONTENTS

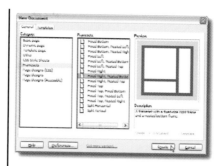

TABLE OF CONTENTS

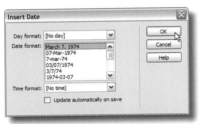

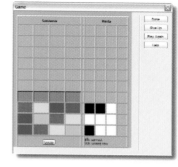

TABLE OF CONTENTS

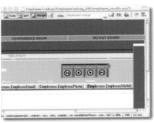

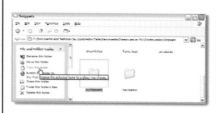

TABLE OF CONTENTS

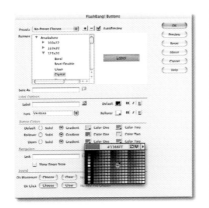

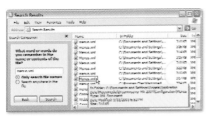

INTRODUCTION

Why we wrote this book

Sitting around the virtual café one day, we had a great idea.

"Hey, we know some stuff," we said to each other, "Maybe the stuff we know could help other folks interested in the same stuff."

"Yeah, but, it's got to be the best stuff, the crème de la crème stuff, the greatest stuff on earth!" we agreed.

"Killer stuff!" we exclaimed simultaneously.

After several Internet-years of research ('bout a week-and-a-half in so-called "real time"), we realized what we had wasn't just a bunch of stuff; it was a full range of time-saving, productivity-enhancing, Dreamweaver MX 2004 tips with an energy efficiency rating of 11.3. You've seen tips like these before, sprinkled through every major Dreamweaver book ever published (and there have been a few), appearing in sidebars or as special asides, typically with cutesy icons created as an exercise in Design 101. Quite often, those tips, notes, and warnings are what really super-charge a book, inspiring all those "Aha" and "Oh, now I get it" responses and the "Why didn't they tell me this earlier?" questions all across the land.

So what makes this book special? Let us count the ways. First, we've dispensed with everything but the tips! You won't have to wade through pages and pages of overviews or feature descriptions to get to the good stuff. Second, we've obliterated all those annoying little icons—just blew 'em to smithereens! They blew up real good.* Third, there's one thing the tips in all those regular Dreamweaver books don't have that we have in abundance: pictures! Full-color figures illustrate nearly every tip—it's the closest thing to a mind meld this side of Vulcan.*

Is This Book For You?

What's that you say—you just need to know one more thing and you'll reach perfect Dreamweaver enlightenment? Then, yes, this is the book for you! This is a book filled with the things you need to know to get the most out of Dreamweaver and use it to build blindingly sharp, cutting-edge websites. All you need to get going with this book is a rudimentary working knowledge of Dreamweaver—if you can perform the basic operations and know your way around the interface, you're good to go.

Remember the *Incredible Shrinking Man*? Well, Dreamweaver is the "incredible growing program," gaining complexity and power with every release—and *Dreamweaver MX 2004 Killer Tips* is your guidebook to all the shortcuts and secret treasures buried there.

Okay, How Do I Get Started?

Take a handkerchief or scarf and fold it a couple of times so that it is about 3 inches wide and opaque. Wrap it around your eyes and tie it at the back of your head like a blindfold. Hold the book in one hand, and flip through the pages with the other hand. At a random moment, stab your finger someplace on one of the pages. Keep your finger where it is and remove the blindfold. (This may take some rubbing of your head up against a wall.) Read the tip your finger is pointing out. Presto—instant knowledge. Repeat about 300 times. Okay, you can just close your eyes instead of using the blindfold, but you'll have much less to talk about if your mother should happen to walk in the room while you're doing this.

The point is (no, not the finger again) that you can start anywhere and read the tips in any order. Although most of the chapters are based on a particular theme, such as CSS or extensibility, the tips themselves are self-contained and don't follow any particular sequence. This means that if you're doing a site using a lot of templates and library items, you might want to focus on Chapter 6, "Assembly-Line Acceleration: Rapid Template and Library Production." Or, you can skim a number of chapters at a time in a personal test of high-geek knowledge. But don't even think about curling up with this book on the sofa—there are way too many good ideas here for you to drift off to sleep.

Is This Book for Macintosh, Windows, or Both?
Yes.

Flip through the book quickly—go on, we'll wait. Notice that about half the pictures are from Macintosh and half from Windows? We know there are Dreamweaver users on both sides of the fence, and we want everyone to feel at home. The two interfaces are close to identical and also represent the different options available in Dreamweaver MX 2004. Where there are differences—mostly in the keyboard shortcuts—we present both options, typically with Windows first and the Macintosh equivalent in parentheses. Hey, what can I tell you? Bill and Steve tossed a coin—a gold Krugerrand, I think, valued at your net worth—and Bill won.

Is There A Website?
Dreamweaver MX 2004 Killer Tips not only has a website, but we're also closing the deal on a reality series for Fox called "Tips!" The theme song goes like this, "Good tips, good tips, what 'cha gonna do? What 'cha gonna do when they read through you?" But, until that airs, you'll just have to visit the site at www.dwkillertips.com to uncover the latest wave of super-cool tips or, if you want, contact the authors to offer us fabulously high-paying jobs with little or no real work involved.

So what are you waiting for? Power up that copy of Dreamweaver MX 2004 and prepare to hit the afterburner switch with *Dreamweaver MX 2004 Killer Tips*.

*Inside jokes—If you don't get 'em, just give a little knowing snort and a minor smirk and nobody will know.

Dreamweaver MX 2004 Killer Tips
Edited by Scott Kelby

Welcome to *Dreamweaver MX 2004 Killer Tips*. As Editor for the Killer Tips series, I can't tell you how excited and truly gratified I am to see this concept of creating a book that is cover-to-cover nothing but tips, extend from my original book (*Photoshop Killer Tips*) into *Dreamweaver MX 2004 Killer Tips*.

The idea for this series of books came to me when I was at the bookstore looking through the latest Photoshop books on the shelf. I found myself doing the same thing to every book I picked up: I'd turn the page until I found a paragraph that started with the word "Tip." I'd read the tip, then I'd keep turning until I found another sidebar tip. I soon realized I was hooked on tips, because I knew that if I were writing the book that's where I'd put all my best material. Think about it: If you were writing a book, and you had a really cool tip, an amazing trick, or an inside secret or shortcut, you wouldn't bury it among hundreds of paragraphs of text. No way! You'd make it stand out: You'd put a box around it, maybe put a tint behind it, and if it was really cool (and short and sweet), you'd get everybody's attention by starting with the word "Tip!"

That's what got me thinking. Obviously, I'm not the only one who likes these tips, because almost every software book has them. There's only one problem: There's never *enough* of them. And I thought, "Wouldn't it be great if there were a book that was nothing but those cool little tips?" (Of course, the book wouldn't actually have sidebars, since what's in the sidebars would be the focus: nothing but cool shortcuts, inside secrets, slick ways to do the things we do everyday, but faster—and more fun— than ever!) That was the book I really wanted, and thanks to the wonderful people at New Riders, that's the book they let me write (along with my co-author and good friend Felix Nelson). It was called *Photoshop Killer Tips*, and it became an instant bestseller because Felix and I were committed to creating something special: A book where every page included yet another tip that would make you nod your head, smile, and think "Ahhh, so that's how they do it."

TIP

If you were writing a book, and you had a really cool tip, an amazing trick, or an inside secret or shortcut, you wouldn't bury it among hundreds of paragraphs of text. You'd make it stand out: You'd put a box around it, maybe put a tint behind it, and if it was really cool (and short and sweet), you'd get everybody's attention by starting with the word "Tip!"

If you've ever wondered how the pros get twice the work done in half the time, it's really no secret: They do every- thing as efficiently as possible. They don't do *anything* the hard way. They know every timesaving shortcut, every workaround, every speed tip, and as such they work at full speed all the time. They'll tell you, when it comes to being efficient, and when it comes to staying ahead of the com- petition: Speed Kills!

Well, what you're holding in your hand is another Killer Tips book:

A book packed cover-to-cover with nothing but those cool little sidebar tips (without the sidebars). Joseph Lowery and Angela Buraglia have once again captured the spirit and flavor of what a Killer Tips book is all about. I can't wait for you to get into it, so I'll step aside and let them take the wheel, because you're about to get faster, more efficient, and have more fun in Dreamweaver MX 2004 than you ever thought possible.

Have fun and enjoy the ride!

All my best,

Scott Kelby, Series Editor

Well-Oiled Machine

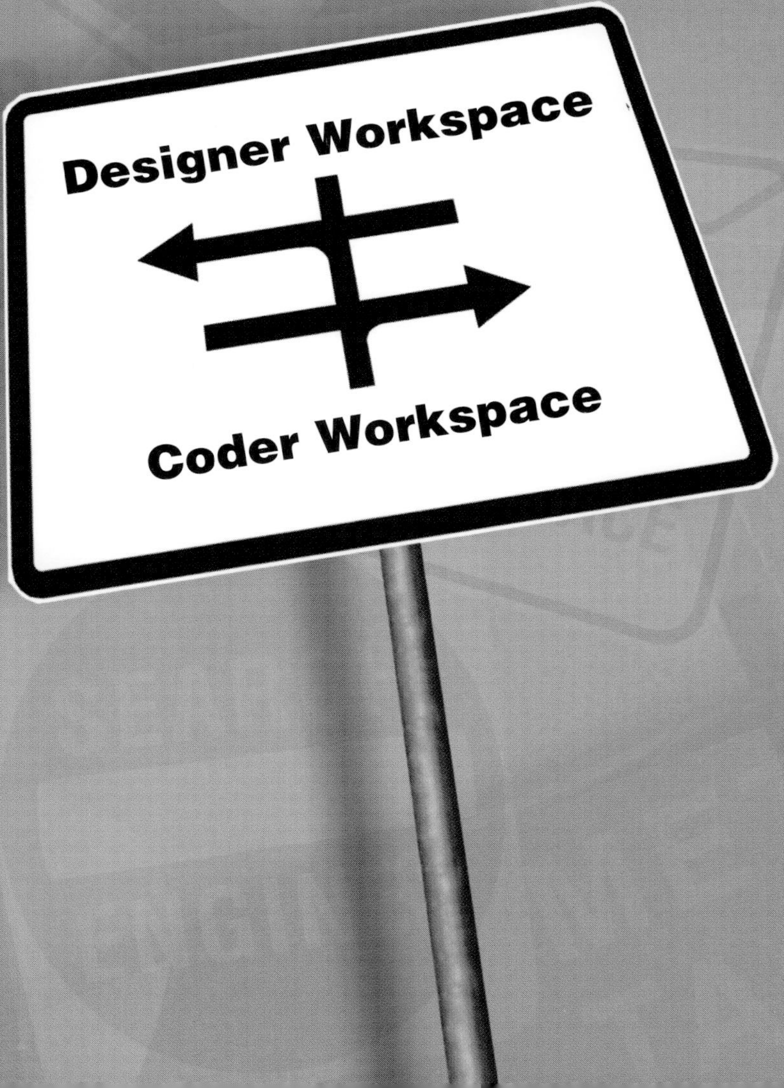

"We're here at the Web Development Racing Championships play-offs, speaking with the sport's rising star, Webifyin' Jones. Tell me, Webifyin', what gives you your edge?"

Well-Oiled Machine:

Working the Dreamweaver Workspace

"It's all in the machine, Pat, all in the machine. I'm just there to guide it."

"And guide it you do. So, tell me about your tool, then. What do you have under the hood?"

"It's Dreamweaver MX 2004, Pat. Straight out of the box."

"I don't know about that, Webifyin'...looks like you did a fair bit of customization on that puppy."

"That's the beauty of it, Pat. I can shape Dreamweaver to work the way I want to work and really max out its performance. Whether I'm laying it down in Design mode or cruising in Code view, Dreamweaver helps me give the best that I've got."

"I notice you seem to have some sort of manual you're clutching. Is that your secret weapon?"

"I'm sorry, but I can't reveal all my sources, Pat. I will say, however, that the first chapter of this book is really a killer when it comes to squeezing the most performance out of Dreamweaver's workspace. It's got more tips on working with panels, toolbars and shortcuts than I ever thought possible. Just thinking about it gets my engines revving."

"Thank you Webifyin' and good luck."

  DECIDING ON WORKSPACE

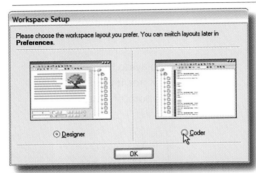

If you're a Windows user, the first time you started Dreamweaver you were presented a choice of workspace. Let's compare those two workspaces. The Designer workspace has the panels grouped on the right. The Coder workspace opens in Code view and has panels grouped on the left. Okay, so there are a few other minor differences, but nothing all that significant. So what's the difference? I'm telling you that there really is none!

The Workspace dialog is just a Dreamweaver Preference setting that is intended as a workspace starting point. Customize your workspace any way you like. With either workspace, you can choose the document view (Code, Design, or Split, which shows both Code and Design view in one document window). Despite the chosen workspace, you can drag Panel groups and dock them on the left or right sides of the Document window. You read that correctly; you can have Panel groups on both sides! To dock a Panel group, click and drag the Panel group by its gripper and release it when the Panel group is in position. (An outline appears when you've hit the sweet spot.) Centered on the divider between the Panel groups and the document area is an expand/collapse arrow that collapses the width/height of the Panel groups. Check out the illustration; I bet you can't tell which workspace it started as originally.

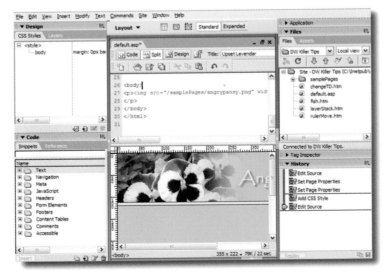

QUICK HYPERLINKS

Walk up behind me and chances are you'll find the Files panel collapsed displaying the Local view. If it is not, it is just a keyboard shortcut away (F8). I like to keep it ready so that I can use it to make quick hyperlinks using the point-to-file system. I'm not just talking about the little folder with target icons you'll find for making hyperlinks; there's one little known way to add hyperlinks the point-to-file way. First, select some text in Design view. Then, while holding the Shift key and clicking the mouse on or near the selection, drag to any file listed in the Local View of the Files panel. If that's not slick, I don't know what is!

MORE FONTS PLEASE

I've never been satisfied with the default list of fonts that Dreamweaver provides in various dialogs and the Property inspector. By choosing Text > Font > Edit Font List, you can create your own font lists or rearrange the order of existing lists. Remember that browsers will look for fonts in the order they appear, so it is always a good idea to end the list with serif or sans serif as a catchall. You're not limited to fonts on your system either; you can type the name of any font—whether or not it is listed—in the field below the available fonts list. After you've created your font list, you'll find it listed in all the usual spots, including code hints for CSS.

  COME BACK, SITE MENU, COME BACK!

Okay, the Site menu was getting kind of long and unruly and, in the current Dreamweaver version has been significantly curtailed. Is that functionality— quick access to File View columns, the Site Map, and Contribute administration—lost forever? Of course not, it's just been relocated to a more exclusive neighborhood. Err … make that hoods, 'cause it's in two places.

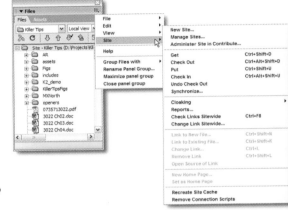

If you're working with the Files panel in its collapsed state, the Site menu is a hop and a skip away. Make sure you've got a site selected (and not one of your local drives or server connections) from the Files panel drop-down list, and then choose the Options menu. Lookee there—it's the Site menu! If you've got the expanded Files panel open, the Site menu is there, front and (slightly to the right of) center. Welcome back, `<ducking>` you're a site for sore eyes! `</ducking>`

   LOCAL FILES, WHEREFORE ART THOU?

The more I use Dreamweaver, the more I look for ways to avoid going to other programs for simple tasks, such as locating a file. In Dreamweaver MX, the Macromedia engineers integrated local file access in the Files panel. Icons for the desktop and other local computer nodes were right next to your currently chosen site. But now, those icons are missing—can you still get access? You bet your sweet bippy*, you can.

Check out the drop-down list in the Files panel. In addition to listing all your sites and siteless connections, this list offers access to local drives and categories such as Desktop (Computer). The local drives are listed above all the Dreamweaver-defined connections. Make your choice, and the files and folders are displayed in the Files panel, available for the picking!

*Really archaic (c. 1968) pop-culture reference, now considered post-post-retro. Use at your own risk.

HIDE-N-SEEK PANELS

Sometimes when you're working on a layout in Design view, you really need to see the full picture. Let's face it; panels take up a lot of valuable horizontal and vertical space! Whenever you want to rid your workspace of all panels, you can toggle them on and off by pressing the F4 key. If you're the menu-using type, you'll find Window > Hide Panels or Window > Show Panels just as useful. To get the document to full screen, Windows users need to maximize the document only if it wasn't maximized already when F4 was pressed, but Macintosh users must always manually maximize the document. If you have a mouse that lets you assign keyboard shortcuts to the scroll wheel, this is a good one!

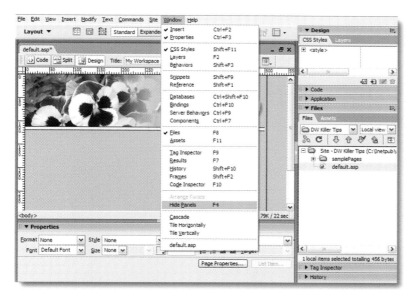

   CLOSE 'EM DOWN, JOE

It's a rare day in Cucamunga when I'm working on just one document in Dreamweaver. I might be moving a recordset from one page to another or comparing layouts in a static site or tweaking a style sheet and checking out the results. Whatever the workload, you can be sure I've got a load of files open at the same time. If you work the same way, there's another chore ahead of you when it comes to quitting time: closing all those docs. In previous versions of Dreamweaver, you had to close each one individually. Well, Windows users had no choice but to take the long, hard road—Mac folk could always Option+Click the close widget of any document to close them all. Now folks in both camps can get out of Dodge immediately by choosing File > Close All. Now you can kick back just a wee bit sooner than before.

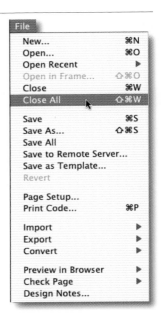

   OPEN 'EM BACK UP, MOE

Working with a bunch of documents over a long haul just got tons easier. You've seen how you can close all your open docs with one swift click (assuming you've read the "Close 'em Down, Joe" tip). But how about the times when you're in the middle of a work session and you need to quit Dreamweaver (heaven forbid!) and come back later. Previously, you had to go through the laborious process of re-opening all your docs to set up your work environment properly. Now, Dreamweaver will do it for you—if you know two simple tricks.

The first trick is to enable the re-open option in Preferences. Go into Edit > Preferences and, from the General category, check the Reopen Documents on Startup option. Now here's the second trick: Don't close your documents before you exit Dreamweaver. If you do close them all, you'll either get the start page or an empty, documentless interface. If you leave one or more (or all) of them open before you choose Quit the Program, however, Dreamweaver re-opens them all when the program starts up again. Now that's a tip to beat the tom-toms about.

CONTEXT MENUS

Context menus are all over the place in the Dreamweaver environment, often in places you may not think to try. What you see all depends on what is selected or in focus at the time you trigger the context menu. Did you know that most keyboards have a context menu key? They vary in location from keyboard to keyboard, but the icon found on the key is somewhat of a standard. Look for an icon that looks like a menu with an arrow pointing to an option. If for some reason the context menu key doesn't do the trick or if you prefer to use your mouse, you can right-click (Ctrl+Click) just about anywhere and expect to see a context menu. You can even find some commands in context menus that you can't find anywhere else in the interface. The moral of the story is this: Look for context menus everywhere you can in Dreamweaver and get familiar with their options to improve your workflow.

   ## STANDARD TOOLBAR

Sometimes the simplest of features can please the masses, and this is certainly in that category. The Standard toolbar offers—at the touch of a button—the typical commands you would find in most any program: New Document, Open, Save, Save All, Cut, Copy, Paste, Undo, and Redo. The same commands found on the Standard toolbar are also located in either the File or Edit menu, but sometimes it is just easier to press a button. By default, the Standard toolbar is turned off. You can display this toolbar two ways: Select View > Toolbars > Standard or right-click (Ctrl+Click) the Document toolbar in an area that is free of buttons or fields or right-click (Ctrl+Click) on the Insert bar to the right of all icons and choose Standard from the context menu.

  TOOLBAR SANDWICH, YUMMM!

Some people put their peanut butter on the left side of a PB and J sandwich, whereas others are righties. Some folks like their toolbars attached to the Document window, others don't. No matter which camp you fall in, now you can have it your way—with toolbars as well as sandwiches. By default, all toolbars open as part of the Document window, right below the document tabs when the doc is maximized. If your files are not maximized, the toolbars go right below the Insert bar. See that? Now, go back to a maximized state—did you know you can drag the toolbar from the Document window and place it under the Insert bar? Now it will be in that position regardless of whether your windows are maxed out. Heck, you can even put one toolbar under the Insert bar and another, such as the Standard one, under the Document window. Now you have yourself a nice toolbar sandwich, with a Document window filling. All very tasty—of course, the meatiest part of this tip is that you can now move toolbars wherever you'd like.

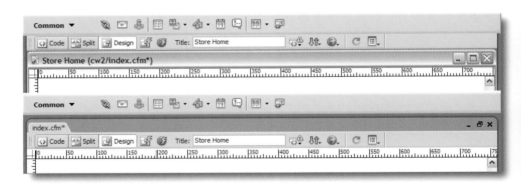

    ## TIME TO PLAY FAVORITES

Although there's a good chance you'll use most of the objects on the Insert bar at one point, if you're like me there are some you use way more than any of the others. Now you don't have to go digging for your MFOs (most frequent objects—pronounced "mofo's"), you can just choose Favorites. Favorites is a new customizable category of the Insert bar. Any object available in any of the standard Insert bar categories (and then some) can be made a Favorite. To get started with customizing your Insert bar, choose the Favorites category. Then right-click (or Ctrl+Click) on the Insert bar itself and select Customize Favorites. (Psst… a little bird told me that you can bring up Customize Favorites from anywhere on the Insert bar.) The Customize Favorite Objects dialog pops up with a full list on the left of all the objects you can access. The top-most list enables you to quickly limit your options to a particular category such as Forms, or you can go through them all. After you've found one you want, select the double-arrow button and the object is transferred to the Favorites side. After you've done a few, you might want to add a separator to group them more effectively or use the up and down arrows to re-order them; the objects listed top to bottom appear left to right. If you accidentally choose the wrong object, remove it from the Favorites list by selecting it and clicking the trashcan icon. Click OK to see your MFOs front and center. Feel free to revise Favorites at any time by bringing up the dialog via the ol' right-click (Ctrl+Click).

  TAKING MEASURES

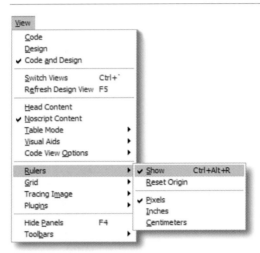

By default, the rulers start at 0 in the upper left of the Document window. If you've set your page margins to a value other than 0, you may want the rulers to start where your page starts. You can adjust the rulers by dragging the ruler-origin icon (located where the horizontal and vertical rulers meet in the upper-left corner of the Document window) to the desired coordinates. You'll see a set of crosshairs that indicate the origin position relative to the page. To return the origins to their default values, just double-click the ruler-origin icon and they'll snap back into place.

Use the View > Rulers submenu to toggle the rulers on and off, reset the origin (as described previously), or change their unit of measurement to pixels (the default), inches, or centimeters.

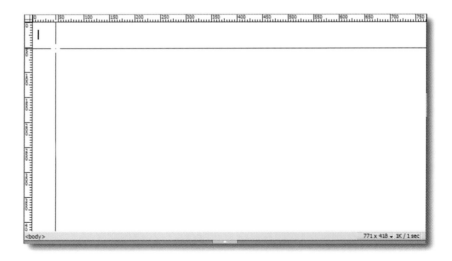

PLOTTING THE GRID

When you are designing with absolute positioned `<div>` tags—known as Layers in Dreamweaver—or even just absolute positioned elements in general, you will find that the grid can come in very handy. Choose View > Grid > Show Grid or press Ctrl+Alt+G (Command+Option+G) to toggle the grid on and off. The default grid is set to 50-pixel increments in a tan color. This default setting may not be useful for your particular design, especially if you'll be taking advantage of the Snap to Grid feature (also enabled via the View > Grid submenu).

By now, you should have noticed there is a third entry in the View > Grid submenu: Grid Settings. Grid Settings lets you alternately enable and disable the grid itself or the snapping feature; create your grid in the color you want; use pixels, centimeters, or inches; and display the grid as lines or dots. I have found that when the increment is smaller than the default—for example, 20 pixels or less—lines tend to be a better choice because they are easier on the eyes than a bunch of tiny little dots. When I need a larger grid, I like to use dots so that I'm not distracted by the solid lines. If you're using inches, you can even enter decimal values, such as .75 for a 3/4-inch measurement. Don't forget to click the Apply button to see your choices in action, and after you're satisfied, click OK.

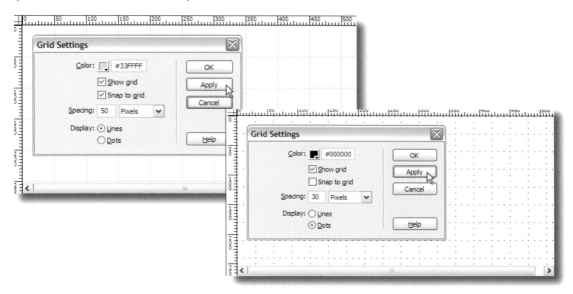

   ONE AND ONLY

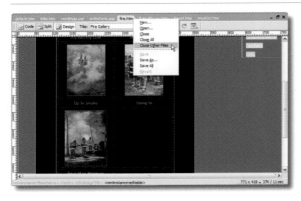

Sometimes when I'm working, I find myself overwhelmed by the multitude of open files. There's usually one file I need to keep open however, so using the "Close 'em Up, Joe" tip (also in this chapter) isn't quite what I need. Macromedia took the idea of closing documents one step further and introduced Close Other Files for Windows users (sorry Macintosh users!). For this tip to work, you must have a document

maximized so that there are filename tabs at the top of the Document window. Bring the document you want to keep open to focus if it isn't already, and then right-click the document's filename tab and choose Close Other Files. All but the current document will close. I don't know about you, but I work much more efficiently without all those extra documents staring at me.

   MY ASSET IS YOUR ASSET

The more sites you develop, the more you'll find elements they have in common. Instead of spending time re-creating things such as 1×1-pixel transparent GIF images or taking the time to hunt down an asset in one site just to copy it to another site, right-click (Ctrl+Click) the asset you want to copy to another site—it doesn't matter which category of the Assets panel you're in—and then select the site listed in the Copy to Site submenu. Oh, but it gets better: You don't have to copy one asset at a time to a site. Within each category of the Assets panel, you can select as many assets as you need to copy. Just click the first asset, and then hold the Shift key while clicking the last asset in a contiguous list, or hold the Ctrl (Command) key while clicking individual assets in the list. Then use the context menu as described previously to select a site to copy the assets. After Dreamweaver finishes copying, an alert displays the results of the action—usually that the assets have been successfully copied to the site and can be found in the Favorites section of the Assets panel for that site.

ZOOM ZOOM ZOOM

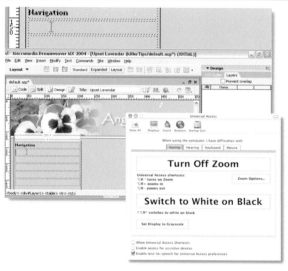

Every now and then, I find that I need to zoom in on something in Dreamweaver to get a closer look. Wouldn't it be cool to have a zoom button like in Fireworks? Well, you don't really need one in Dreamweaver because chances are your operating system has a magnification utility built in. On Windows, look in the Programs menu for Accessories > Accessibility > Magnifier.

On Macintosh, look in Apple Menu > System Preferences and click Universal Access in the System section. Now just click the Turn On Zoom

in big bold type. You'll find these tools prove quite handy for use inside Dreamweaver and in your general everyday workflow.

DON'T WAIT FOR ME, FTP!

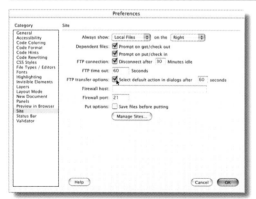

Dreamweaver is loaded with lots of little time savers, but this is one of the few with which you can specify the time being saved. Have you ever started an FTP session to transfer a slew of files and decided to take a break—only to come back 10 minutes later and see a dialog on the screen asking permission to overwrite the second file in the queue? Very frustrating. With Dreamweaver's FTP, such dialog's default action (typically OK) can be automatically accepted after a set number of seconds. Check out the Site

category of Preferences, in the File Transfer Options area. If you check the Select Default Actions in Dialogs option, you can set how long you want Dreamweaver to wait before proceeding. Now, go enjoy that break while Dreamweaver does all the heavy lifting—you deserve it!

   SPLITTING THE FILES PANEL

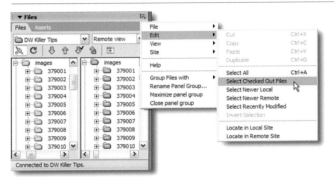

Some folks may think this trick qualifies as a "bug," but I like to think of it as an "undocumented feature." You may want to view remote and local files at the same time in the docked Files panel, but there is no option to do so if the Files panel is collapsed\ docked. For some reason, Macromedia decided that the Expand\Collapse button was all that we needed. When I first came across this "feature," I did a celebratory chair dance because Macromedia said it just couldn't be done. (Now you're wondering which one of us wrote this tip. Shame on you. It wasn't that kind of dance.)

First you have to enable Check In/Check Out in the site definition if it isn't already set up. Then you switch to Remote view, click the Files panel's Options menu, and choose Edit > Select Checked Out Files. Just don't expand the Files panel without switching back to Local view or you'll have just the Local view showing while it is expanded. If that happens to you, just collapse the Files panel again and expand it if needed. To think, they said it just couldn't be done!

   LOCATING FILES

Dreamweaver conveniently displays the folder name and filename in the title bar of open documents. Because it is possible that you could have multiple folders within your site that have the same name, seeing only one folder level in the path to the file in the title bar isn't always enough. No more digging through each folder trying to find where the current file belongs; Site > Locate in Site will find the current document in the Files panel and select it for you. If the file you've selected is not in the current site that is listed in the Files panel, don't bother switching sites first because Dreamweaver will switch to the correct site for you.

BYPASS OBJECT DIALOG BOXES

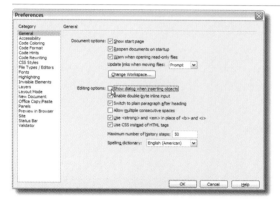

You can disable the Show Dialog when Inserting Objects check box in the General category of Preferences. With this option checked, only dialogs that absolutely require input display. Accessibility dialogs, if enabled, in your Accessibility preferences always show despite bypassing the main object dialog. If a dialog is not shown, the default values for the object are inserted into the code for that object.

I prefer to allow the dialogs to always be shown, and instead bypass dialogs on a case-by-case basis. To do that, all you need to do is Ctrl+Click (Command+Click) an object and the dialog will be bypassed just as it would have been had you disabled the preference. Dreamweaver stores the information each time you fill out an object dialog, so that the next time you insert that object it is populated with your previous usage's values. You can bypass the dialog of many objects, but not all of them, so feel free to explore each object to see the result of your bypass attempts.

   ## NEXT DOCUMENT PLEASE

Moving from document to document doesn't require you to use your mouse. Similar to how you can Alt+Tab (Option+Tab) between different programs or windows in your taskbar, Dreamweaver offers a shortcut for moving between documents: Ctrl+Tab (Command+Tab). Use the shortcut whenever you have a Document window in focus, and the next document in line will be brought to the front. Add the Shift key to the combo and you'll move backward through the file lineup.

   TILING WINDOWS

When I need to see all documents onscreen at the same
time so that I can compare
them line by line, I choose
Window > Tile Horizontally to
set up documents side by side
or Window > Tile Vertically so
that the documents are set up
one above the other.
Unfortunately, if you're a Mac
user you won't have that
option; Mac users must arrange
documents manually. Here's
what you need to know: You
can tile up to three documents
horizontally or vertically. Four
documents will be laid out the
same, no matter what your
choice, and any more than that,
well, I'll just let you figure it out.
If you've minimized a docu-
ment, it won't be included in
the tiling. After you've tiled the
documents to your liking, you
can easily compare them or
copy/paste between them. I
also like to tile documents
when I need to use the color
picker in one document and
choose the color from another.

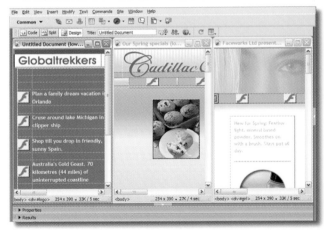

FILES BY DATE

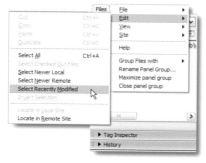

You've seen the Open Recent list of files in the File menu plenty of times, but that only lists the 10 most recent files and it is not site based. What if you want to open all the files you worked on yesterday in a particular site? That's where the nifty new Select Recently Modified Files feature comes in very handy. You can access Select Recently Modified Files from either the Edit menu of the expanded Files panel (on Windows only), or from the Options menu under Edit on the collapsed Files panel. The dialog offers you two ways to select files; you can choose between files modified within a certain number of days or files modified in a range of dates. When you run the command, all the files that meet your criteria are selected for you in the Files panel. To open them, right-click (Ctrl+Click) one of the selected files and choose Open from the context menu. You can upload the selected files, delete them, and even do a search within them by using the Ctrl+F (Command+F) keyboard shortcut, or choose another file operation from the context or Options menu.

MAXIMUM PANEL HEIGHT

Double-clicking the Panel group title bar is just a little quicker than using the Options menu to choose Maximize Panel Group. This will minimize all other expanded Panel groups (if any) within the docking area and expand the current Panel group to the maximum available height.

  SAME SHORTCUTS GET ANY PANEL YOU WANT!

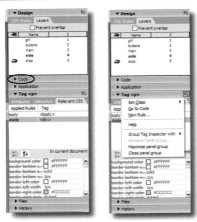

Sorry Mac users, this tip is for Windows only. Each panel has its very own keyboard shortcut—all of which are listed beside their entry in the Window menu. You really don't need to know every single panel shortcut. As long as you know a few easy shortcuts, you can get to any panel you need. Ctrl+Alt+Tab gives focus to the first Panel group, indicated by dashed lines around the Panel group title. Each time you press the shortcut, you move focus to the next Panel group. Use Ctrl+Alt+Shift+Tab to move backward through the Panel groups.

Use the spacebar to toggle the Panel group between closed and expanded. If a Panel group is already expanded, you can tab to the Options menu and view its menu by pressing the spacebar. Use your up and down arrow keys to move through the list, and then press Enter to make a selection.

If there are multiple panels in a Panel group, use Ctrl+Tab to get to the one you want. Toss in the Shift key to move backward if you feel the need. Press just the Tab key to move between options in the given panel. Generally, you'll use the spacebar to press buttons, the up and down arrow keys to move through lists, and Enter to make a selection. If your mouse breaks, you're prepared!

SKIPPING FROM SITE TO SITE

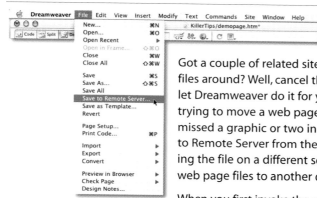

Got a couple of related sites and you want to move some files around? Well, cancel that U-Haul rental reservation and let Dreamweaver do it for you. We all know the danger of trying to move a web page and discovering that we've missed a graphic or two in the process. By choosing Save to Remote Server from the File menu, you're not only storing the file on a different server, you're also copying the web page files to another defined site.

When you first invoke the command, you'll see the current site's remote files listed. To see a list of other defined sites and servers, choose Websites from the Save In drop-down list or click the Up One Level icon. Double-click any site or server to open it and locate a new home for your files. When you click Save, Dreamweaver automatically transfers files to both the remote server and your locally defined sites. If there are any dependent files—and you know there are—these are copied and any needed folders are created.

DESIGN ON TOP

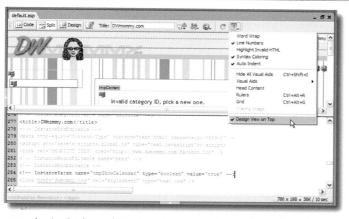

Dreamweaver's workspace is quite flexible. Many workspace layouts are possible so that you can work comfortably and effectively. Not only do you have the option to work in Code and Design views simultaneously, but you also can choose to have Design view on top when working with both views. You must be in Code and Design view already to select View Options > Design View on Top from the Document toolbar.

FASTER SITE OPERATIONS

If you're like me, you prefer to keep your source files (such as Fireworks PNG files and Flash FLA files) in your defined local site so that you always know where to find them. Uploading these files is usually not a good idea because if someone finds them online he may be inclined to use them. Accidentally uploading these files can be avoided with Dreamweaver's cloaking feature.

Cloaking isn't just for source files, but for any folder or file extension that you want to exclude from site operations, which in turn will speed up site operations. Cloaked image files do not appear in the Assets panel, for instance, which improves its load time. Right-click (Ctrl+Click) the folder you want to cloak and select Cloaking > Cloak (unless it is dimmed, in which case you must choose Enable Cloaking instead and then come back and choose Cloak). A red slash indicates that a folder and all files contained in it are now cloaked.

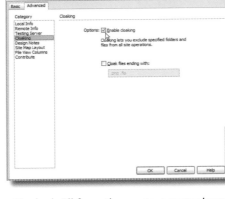

From that same context menu, you can choose Settings, which opens your site definition right to the Cloaking category where you can enable the feature to cloak files with the specified file extension. You can add file extensions to the list separated by a space to tell Dreamweaver which types of files you want to cloak; just be sure to include the dot prior to the extension. All cloaked files are indicated by a red slash through their icon. Be careful if you choose Uncloak All from the context menu because after you do that, if you need the files cloaked again, you'll have to do it manually. It is usually a better choice to just temporarily disable cloaking.

    LOCAL LEFTY, REMOTE RIGHTY

The (expanded) Files panel lists your local site files on the right and remote files on the left. Many FTP clients are set up just the opposite, with your local files on the left and remote on the right. If you're used to that setup, you could get confused and potentially overwrite files, resulting in loss of work. Don't let this happen to you! If you're accustomed to remote files being on the right side, set Dreamweaver up the same way.

To change the Files panel to display local files on the left, select Edit > Preferences (Dreamweaver > Preferences), and then click Site in the list of categories on the left side of the Preferences dialog. Now you should see at the top of the dialog the option that enables you to view local files on the right or left. Changing it to read Always Show Remote Files on the Left is the same as leaving it set to Always Show Local Files on the Right, so you should change only one list value and not the other. Otherwise, the Files panel will remain the same. Click OK to close the dialog.

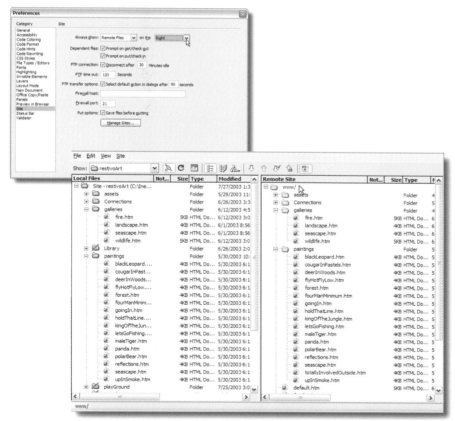

   INSERT TAB A INTO MENU B

Did your heart skip a beat when you saw the new menu-driven Insert bar and instantly fall in love? Or did you go into cardiac arrest because the Insert bar tabs had vanished? Fear not—whichever way your desire leads, the user interface of your dreams awaits. To go back to the tab-based Insert bar, choose the category menu (one last time!) and choose Show as Tabs. Should you then find you actually prefer the new menu style, choose the Insert bar Options button and select Show as Menu. Isn't love grand?

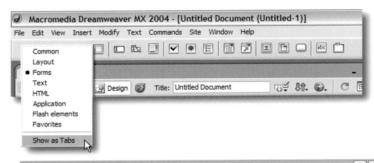

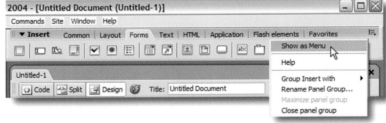

   INSTANT BROWSER CHECKING

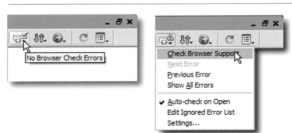

Need an instant indication of browser errors or lack thereof? Now you only need look as far as the Document toolbar to see whether your code lives up to the browser standards you set up (or the defaults set by Dreamweaver). You'll see an icon to the right of the Title field in the Document toolbar that has a checkmark if your code is up to par, or an exclamation mark if it isn't. Click the icon and choose Settings to set up the Target Browser dialog with your browser-checking preferences.

PAGE PROPERTY-PALOOZA

Suddenly it's raining Page Property dialogs. Of course you know that you can begin to alter your general page settings by choosing Modify > Page Properties. Maybe you even knew that pressing the keyboard shortcut Ctrl-J (Command-J) would get you there. But how many of you knew that the same dialog is almost always available through the context menu, just a right-click (Control-click) away? If those three methods weren't enough, a Page Properties button is available on the lower portion of the Text Property inspector, which—as the default Property inspector—is available most of the time.

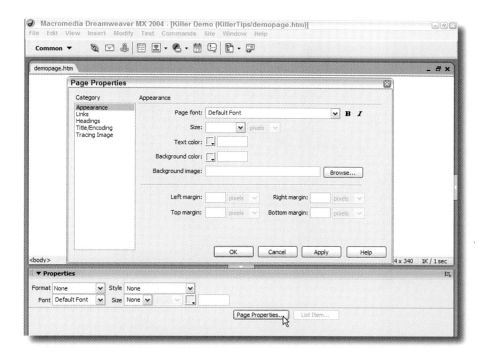

Racehorse
Style

*Now that Dreamweaver MX 2004 is all
snazzed up in its CSS (Cascading Style Sheet)
finery, I bet you want to take it strutting
around town. This chapter is just the ticket seeing*

Racehorse Style:

CSS Power Pointers

*how it is packed with all sorts of cool CSS tricks.
Some tips work in older browsers and some do not;
the cooler the tip, the more likely it is only for modern browsers such as Internet Explorer 5+, Netscape
6+, and Safari. Keep in mind that it is rare that someone — other than web developers or clients — will
see your page in both older browsers and modern
ones; typically, the general public uses only one
browser or another and will never compare the site
between browsers. Don't drive yourself crazy making
everything identical across browsers or platforms.
All that really matters is that the site looks acceptable and is fully functional.*

*You're on your own to test drive the CSS in the
browsers that matter most to you and use them
where appropriate. For the most part, we're not
going to worry about what is or is not proprietary
CSS or "valid" to CSS standards. My goal is to open
you up to the possibilities that CSS has to offer.
Although a few of these tips may be ahead of their
time and not practical for you now, I'm betting they
will prove valuable to you in the future.*

   DESIGN TIME STYLE SHEETS

Design Time style sheets has to be in my top 10, shall we say "sub-merged," features of Dreamweaver. If you've ever opened Server-Side Includes (SSIs) or Library Items that use CSS, you'll know that in Design view, you can't see the applied CSS or make use of the CSS Styles panel. This qualifies as a major bummer in my view.

As long as the document has been previously saved, you may choose the CSS panel's Options menu to select Design Time. You also can right-click (Command+Click) in the CSS Styles panel to display the same Design Time option. When the Design Time Style Sheets dialog box appears, you can click the Add (+) button to browse to and select the CSS file you need. You can even choose to exclude CSS files that are already linked to the file so that they are not shown in Design view, but because they are still part of the code, will show in the browser. You can search through the document if you like, but you won't see any reference to the CSS file in the code at all. In addition to SSIs and Library Items, Design Time style sheets also come in handy when a style sheet is dynamically assigned.

   @IMPORT TRICK

In regards to CSS, there is a simple way to avoid the hassles of browser sniffing and redirects to multiple versions of the same site. What you need to do is have a style sheet that works well for all browsers, and one that contains CSS for modern browsers in a second style sheet called upon @import. Older browsers such as Netscape 4.x do not recognize @import and completely ignore it. This means you can put all the cool CSS into that style sheet and essentially hide it from Netscape 4.x. When you attach a style sheet using Dreamweaver, you will see a radio button option for Link or Import. The procedure is as simple as choosing the CSS file, selecting the Import option, and clicking OK.

Keep in mind that the @import style sheet should come after a linked style sheet so that you can override CSS that was written to satisfy older browsers, with the CSS that is in your @import CSS file.

   EASY BAKE CSS-P

There's just no doubt that Dreamweaver MX 2004 has shown tremendous improvements in the area of CSS to previous versions of Dreamweaver. I was pleasantly surprised to see that there are even six new "Page Designs" that use CSS positioning (also known as CSS-P). Select File > New and in the New Document dialog you'll find the Page Design (CSS) category. A list of six different layouts will appear in the list on the right. After you select the layout you like

and click Create, you'll be prompted to save the document and then you'll be asked to save the dependant CSS and other files. After you've done this, you'll be able to customize the layout however you like by modifying the CSS file and replacing the placeholder content with your own. Studying and changing the CSS file while viewing the results is a great way to learn about CSS-P.

   PLAYING STYLES CLOSE TO THE VEST IN CONTRIBUTE

Hey, buddy! I got some groovy CSS styles to lay on you. Thing is, I don't want 'em to get around—especially to those Contribute users. So what you have to do is hide them. That way only you and I will know they're being used. Those Contribute folks won't be able to see them in their Dreamweaver-designed pages and can't mistakenly apply them. The secret to hiding CSS styles in Contribute is to prefix any style with mmhide_; for example, if you have a custom style named .rufus, you can hide it by renaming it .mmhide_rufus.

   DOUBLE TEAM 'EM WITH CSS CLASSES

Looking for a way to trim some fat from your CSS pages? Take advantage of the modern browser's capability to render multiple classes. Suppose you've got three types of headings in your document: 1) red colored, 2) right justified, and 3) red, right justified. At first glance, you'd think you'd have to declare a CSS selector for each heading, right? Not so, my fellow geek! You only have to create two—one for the color and one for the alignment. The third one can be created by using the other two styles together.

For example, let's call our initial styles .redHead and .rightHead. To make a given `<h1>` tag both red and right justified, we'd use code like this:

```
<h1 class="redHead rightHead">I'm so Red, I'm Right!</h1>
```

Multiple class support is found in Internet Explorer 5+, Netscape 6+, Mozilla, and Opera 7 … and this little web authoring tool you may have heard of … WeaveDreamer. No, that's not it. Hang on, I'll remember in a moment!

COMPUTER CLONING

Recently I discovered that with a little bit of CSS I could make a web page closely resemble that of the user's very own computer. Start your wheels turning and think of the possibilities this brings you! Many computer users will set their system in such a way that is most comfortable for them, especially the visually impaired. Any color or background color can be assigned a system color value. For example, try this code:

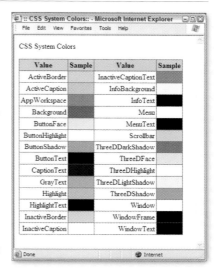

```
body {
background-color: Background;
}
```

The background of your page should now match your system's background color. There's too many possible values to list and describe here, but you can find all of them here: http://www.dwkillertips.com/go/18. Be sure to test your results in various system themes. Did I mention you have to hand-code these values? The Dreamweaver CSS Style Definition dialog will tell you that whatever value you entered is not a valid color, even though it really is! Just click OK on the alert and it will be added to your styles. Oh, and don't expect to see these values represented in Design view.

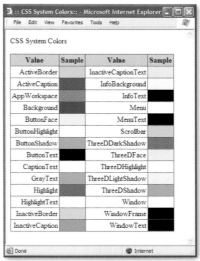

  CAN I SEE SOME IDENTIFICATION PLEASE?

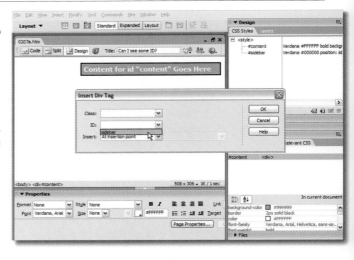

Just about any HTML element can be given an ID attribute to be used in conjunction with CSS to style that element. ID values must be unique to the document; you can't use the same ID more than once on a page or you'll run into trouble. CSS offers what is known as ID selectors that automatically apply the CSS to the ID that matches it. Take this code, for example:

```
#content {
color: #333333;
}
```

In the document, you could have something like this:

```
<p id="content">Some text here</p>
```

That particular paragraph would display with the color specified by the `content ID` defini-tion. With this method, you can ensure that no other element is presented in the same way, because the ID must be unique and will not get used by another tag. Another good thing about this method is that it prevents your coworkers—or yourself—from applying the wrong CSS to an element if it had just been written as a custom class instead.

To add an ID selector through Dreamweaver's interface, select the Selector Type: Advanced radio button and enter a # followed by the ID in the Selector field at the top of the dialog. Click OK, and then define your CSS. If you've already got IDs for `<div>`s in your CSS file, you'll even get a list of the unused IDs in the drop-down list in the Insert Div Tag object. Better yet, Dreamweaver only shows those IDs in the style sheet that have not yet been assigned.

       ## PSSST ... NEED A STYLISH HINT?

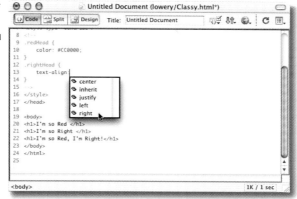

If you've been doing any sort of manual coding with Dreamweaver you're probably familiar with code hints. You know, you're laying down some heavy code and a momentary brain freeze blocks the needed attribute from coming through the mental maze. Suddenly, Dreamweaver provides you with a full list of applicable hints. Because tweaking CSS is more and more part of the job description these days, you'll be happy to know that Dreamweaver now has code hints for CSS, too! Can't remember all the applicable values? Just enter the colon after the CSS property and wait a sec—bam! There they are. Finish off the property with a semicolon, and all the rest of the properties are there for you to choose from. If they don't appear, you can force the hints to show by pressing Ctrl+Spacebar (Cmd+Spacebar).

       ## /* STRIPPER */

It is easy to get carried away and make a lot of comments in CSS files, especially when I create CSS files for other developers. Next to each custom class, I usually place a comment for them describing its purpose and its allowed usage within the site and perhaps any browser support issues. I also tend to break up the file, keeping rules of similar nature near each other, separated by a CSS comment such as /* Table Styles */ or /* Form styles */. This can get lengthy, and we don't want the site visitors to wait a second longer than they have to because of verbose CSS comments.

One way you can trim load time off a site is to remove CSS comments. I suggest keeping a local copy of the CSS file with comments intact and uploading one with comments stripped out. Choose Edit > Find and Replace. You want to Find In the Current Document and Source Code. Use a regular expression in the Find field: \/*[^*]**+([^/][^*]**+)*\/. Let's leave the Replace field blank and make sure the Use Regular Expressions check box is marked. You may want to save this query for future use by clicking the Save icon. Before you click Replace All, make sure you have a backup file, just in case. After you've stripped all the comments, save your CSS file and upload it.

CHAPTER 2 • CSS Power Pointers   33

   CLASSY BUT CAREFUL

Some custom classes would wreak havoc on your design if not properly applied. This can be especially true for the styling of form buttons. Here's an example of CSS that can only be applied to an `<input>` tag with the class attribute equal to `"go"`:

```
input.go {
font:bold 13px Verdana,Arial,Helvetica,sans-serif;
color:#333333;
background:#CDD5DC;
border:1px #06334B outset;
}
```

The syntax for this type of selector is `element.class` or `element#id` and requires that you use the Selector Type: Advanced radio button in the New CSS Styles dialog. So long as the go class is not defined elsewhere in your style sheet, it doesn't matter whether the designer adds `class="go"` to every element on the page. The only element that would be affected by it is the `<input>` tag. That'll teach them designers not to be class-happy! Oh, and just for the record, this is one of those rules you'll want to hide from Netscape 4.x browsers, because of the border.

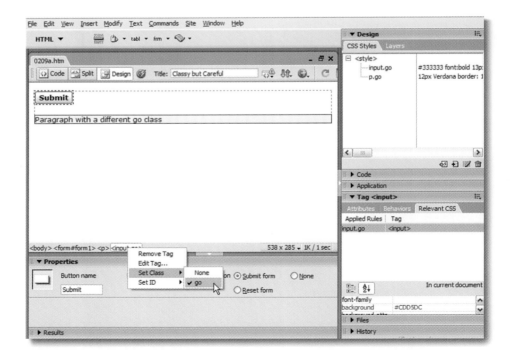

ROUNDING THE CORNERS

Shave off those sharp table edges with a little bit of CSS. That's right—CSS can even round off table corners. The code is proprietary for Mozilla and Netscape 6.x and higher, but it leaves Internet Explorer with normal, sharp tables. You can use Dreamweaver's CSS editor for all but the snippet of code that does the rounding. Create a new style using the Redefine HTML Tag option, and select Table from the list of tags. Proceed as usual to the CSS Style Definition dialog. There you can choose a background color, a border size, and a color for the table. When you're satisfied, click OK. Here's the line of code you need to enter manually at the end of the table style rule you just defined:

```
-moz-border-radius: 12px;
```

Don't forget to add that starting dash, or the code won't work! In Design view, you won't see anything unusual. It's not until you look at the page in a supporting browser that you'll see the rounded corners. The edges can sometimes look jagged, but I find that some colors work better together than others do. I hope that there will be better support for this cool CSS in future browsers.

For extra fun, try this little twist on the same concept, which makes use of a negative value:

```
-moz-border-radius-topright: -12px;
-moz-border-radius-topleft: 10px;
-moz-border-radius-bottomright: 10px;
-moz-border-radius-bottomleft: 10px;
```

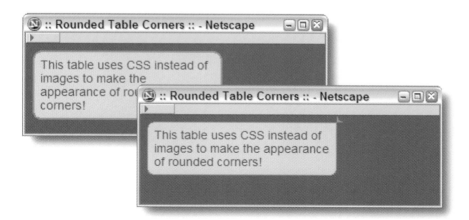

   INSTANT CSS FILE

Who says you must already have a CSS file to link it to the document? Certainly not me! Whichever way you choose to attach a style sheet, be it via the Attach Style Sheet icon, the Attach Style Sheet command in the CSS Styles panel's Options menu or a context menu, or even from the Styles drop-down list in the Property inspector, you'll be prompted by the Link External Style Sheet dialog. Don't worry if you don't already have a CSS file; just type the path to the file as though it already exists and click OK. Dreamweaver will ask you a quick question:

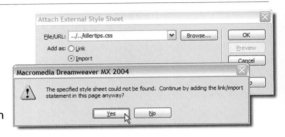

The specified style sheet could not be found. Continue by adding the link/import statement in this page anyway?

Just click Yes and the `<link>` or `@import` statement will be added to your document, and your new CSS file will display in the CSS Styles panel. The first time you create a style for this new style sheet using the New CSS Styles dialog, Dreamweaver creates the physical file in your site. This saves you the time of creating a style sheet first and then coming back to this dialog. You could choose "(New Style Sheet File)" from the Define in dropdown when creating a new style, but then you don't have the option to add the CSS to the document using an @import statement. I love these little timesavers, don't you?

   ## BUSINESS AS USUAL

Just because you prefer to not use inline styles when creating layers—because you've learned the benefits of externalizing your CSS—doesn't mean that you can't take advantage of the fields in the Property inspector for layers. You don't have to edit the external CSS file manually or by using the CSS Style Definition dialog. Dreamweaver doesn't care whether your CSS is inline or external; it is just business as usual. You can modify the values in the Property inspector or drag and adjust the layer itself within the document, and Dreamweaver updates the external CSS file.

Just in case you're a little confused, a layer in Dreamweaver might have an opening tag that looks something like this:

```
<div id="contentLayer" style="position:absolute; left:395px; top:55px;
width:62px; height:45px; z-index:2">
```

You can remove all the values of the style attribute and put them into an external style sheet using an ID selector. If you're working in this fashion, don't forget to upload the external CSS file to see the changes online.

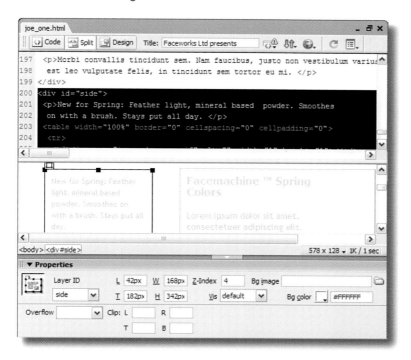

   JUST SNIPPET

There are many properties that the CSS Style Definition dialog doesn't address at all. When you find CSS that Dreamweaver doesn't support, make it into a snippet so that you'll always have it handy. Here's an example of CSS that Dreamweaver doesn't support, colored scrollbars in Internet Explorer 5.5+ on Windows:

```
html{
scrollbar-highlight-color:#C2C2DA;
scrollbar-shadow-color:#8D8DC7;
scrollbar-track-color:#272752;
scrollbar-face-color:#474792;
scrollbar-arrow-color:#E8E8F4;
scrollbar-darkshadow-color:#000000;
scrollbar-3dlight-color:#272752;
}
```

Make your selection in Code view, and then right-click (Ctrl+Click) and choose Create Snippet. Keep in mind that if the CSS Style Definition dialog doesn't have the CSS you need, Dreamweaver won't display it, and it is probably proprietary code that has limited browser support.

   EXPANDED DIV MODE

You may have discovered Dreamweaver's new Expanded Table mode and like myself thought it would be nice to have an Expanded DIV mode as well, so that you could see where all DIVs are at all times and select within them ease as you work. Well, the feature isn't exactly built in for us; with the help of design-time CSS, however, we can achieve similar results. Toss this code in a new CSS file:

```
div{
border: 3px solid red !important;
padding 10px !important;
margin 10px !important;
}
```

To attach the file at design time, open the CSS Styles panel, click the Options menu, and choose Design-Time. Click the Help button if you need more info on design-time CSS. Feel free to change the border, padding, or margin values to your liking.

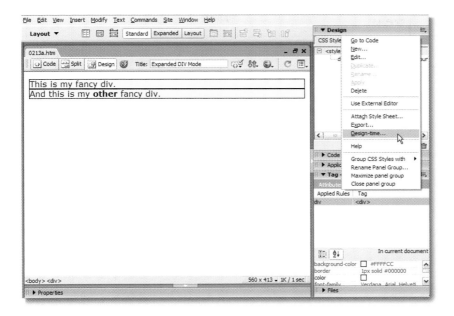

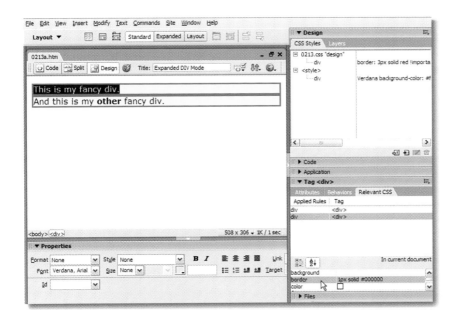

HANDY POINTER

Browser support for the cursor property varies significantly between Internet Explorer and Netscape 6+. What Windows Internet Explorer 5.x knows as the hand, Netscape 6+, Internet Explorer 6, and Macintosh Internet Explorer 5 call the pointer. So how do you make both browsers happy and still get the cursor you desire? It's simple actually. Whenever there is a conflict, the closest style definition wins.

Let's create a custom class called `.mouse`. On the left of the CSS Styles definition dialog, select Extensions. Now select hand from the Cursor drop-down list. In Code view, you need to add `pointer` because Netscape doesn't recognize `hand`, like so:

```
.mouse {
cursor: pointer;
cursor: hand;
}
```

If you flipped that order, Internet Explorer will be looking for `pointer`, which it doesn't understand, and you won't get the desired results. There isn't anything illegal about using the same property twice in a rule. Because the `hand` value is not valid CSS, however, the style sheet won't validate. So use this handy pointer when you think it is appropriate.

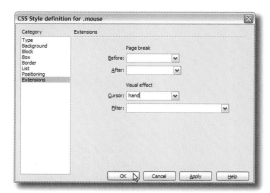

DRIVING ON THE AUTO(STYLE)BAHN

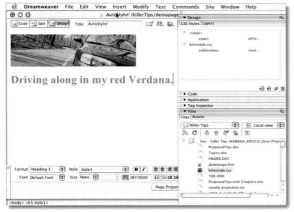

For some, CSS is the grand poobah of Dreamweaver MX 2004. Rendering has been greatly improved and emphasis strongly shifted away from the evil `<font>` tag clan. In fact, there's even a mechanism in place to automagically apply an already defined style, if you choose the same font, color, or size as that style from the Property inspector. Here's how it works: Suppose you've got a class called .redVerdana already defined in an external style sheet. (It also works if the class is set up in the same doc.) The .redVerdana class rule looks like this:

```
.redVerdana {
font-family: Verdana, Arial,
Helvetica, sans-serif;
color: #FF0000;
}
```

Now, suppose an unsuspecting coworker comes along and begins working on a document linked to your style sheet with the .redVerdana class. The coworker is not as CSS savvy as you are, so he selects a paragraph and, instead of choosing .redVerdana from the Style list of the Property inspector like you would, he gives it a red color and chooses the Verdana font family. What does Dreamweaver do? At first, it creates a new class called .style1 (assuming this is his first autocreated style on the page), but then it realizes that the attributes are the same as a defined style. Faster than you can say Carolina Super Sausages, Dreamweaver applies the .redVerdana class to the paragraph and removes the now unneeded .style1. Can you say "slick"?

   COLLAPSING BORDERS

Applying borders to a table and all its cells using CSS isn't entirely simple, as it may seem. Go ahead, create a 3×3 table and try to create the CSS needed to outline each cell with a single pixel line. You can find border options in the Border category of the CSS Style definition dialog. Your first attempt may look something like this if you've set all borders equally and are using shorthand:

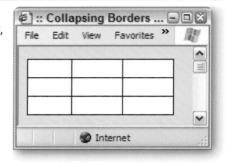

```
table, td, th {
border: 1px solid #000000;
}
```

Both in Dreamweaver and in the browser you will see that borders appear to be two pixels thick, because the borders are on each table cell, and the table cells butt up against each other. To remedy this, just add `border-collapse: collapse;` to the preceding code in Code view—it isn't an option in the CSS Style Definition dialog.

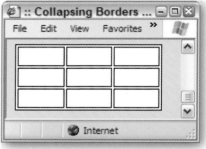

Design view doesn't support it, and if the `<table>` tag doesn't have cell spacing set to zero the lack of support is even more obvious. However, modern browsers such as Internet 5+, Netscape 6+, and Opera 5+ all support the property.

Disclaimer: You may run into some problems if you have empty cells in your table. Other minor caveats may apply. Don't drink and drive. Always wear clean underwear. Void where prohibited by law. Remember to test in the browsers that matter most to you. Eat your vegetables.

  ## A LOVE/HATE RELATIONSHIP

I do whatever it takes to remember coding techniques. I'm not sure who thought of this one originally, but it is simple to remember: LoVe HAte. The capital letters represent the first letter in each of the pseudoclasses used to control hyperlink styles. For the cascade to work as one would normally expect, the order of these pseudoclasses is very important: `a:link`, `a:visited`, `a:hover`, `a:active`. You'll find each one listed in the proper order in the Selector drop-down list when you've chosen Use CSS Selector in the New Style dialog box. In the correct order, one by one, you'll define their rules. When you're finally finished, you should have code similar to the following:

```
a:link {
color: #3C679B;
}
a:visited{
color: #7193BD;
}
a:hover {
color: #274365;
}
a:active{
color: #9771BD;
}
```

Setting them in this order ensures that visited links still use the hover effect.

  CAN'T STOP SEEING CSS?

Now that Dreamweaver has all this great CSS rendering capability, why would you want to turn it off? Looking at a page sans CSS is very helpful when structuring your page for accessibility, especially when it comes to screen readers. It's considered a best practice to place your `<div>` tags in logical sequence in the code, regardless of where they're positioned on the page. In other words, you don't want to put your footer `<div>` above the heading `<div>` (or in your mouth `<div>`). Rendering the page without the CSS manipulations gives you a quick way to check your `<div>` sequence. You can accomplish this in a number of ways. One technique is to select the code that imports or links your external style sheet(s), right-click (Ctrl+Click) and choose Selection > Comment Out Lines from the pop-up menu. Then, switch to Design view to see how you're doing, `<div>`-wise. When you're done, select the CSS lines again and reverse the procedure by choosing Selection > Uncomment Lines.

If you'd rather not go into the code—or can't because it's locked in a template—choose Design-Time from the CSS Styles option menu. When the Design Time Style Sheets dialog opens, add the current style sheets to the Hide at Design Time area. When ready to see your work in all it's glory, open the dialog again and remove the sheets from the Hide field. Now you CSS it, now you don't!

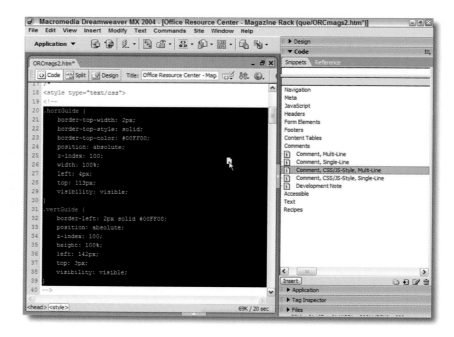

   WHAT THE FOUC?

Sure you've seen the spark of a Wintergreen Life Saver, but have you seen a FOUC? FOUC stands for Flash Of Unstyled Content and is a CSS phenomenon exhibited by Internet Explorer (version 5 or greater) for Windows. You'll know a FOUC when you see one—the page briefly displays with no CSS styling applied; because CSS is increasingly used for lay-out positioning, this can be quite noticeable. First discovered by the nonautomatons at BlueRobot.com, a FOUC occurs when a page imports (rather than links to) an external style sheet. You'll only see the unadorned page once per viewing, however; after the external style sheet is cached, the FOUC vanishes.

How do you banish the unwanted FOUC? Make sure there is a `<link>` tag above your @import CSS rule. Folks who are using a linked style sheet to handle Netscape 4.x are FOUC-less (a minor reward, but still, a reward) as are those who link to another media type for their pages, such as print.

Another option is to link to an empty style sheet—but be extremely careful if you decide to go this route. Make sure that your real style sheet is the one selected in the CSS Styles panel if you add new styles through Dreamweaver's interface. Otherwise, the styles will be insert-ed in your supposedly empty style sheet and you're in for a FOUCing nightmare.

   **BEFORE YOU VIEW, PREVIEW**

Got a mess of CSS style sheets and you're not sure which one should be applied. Dreamweaver enables you to preview your style sheets before you link or import the file. After you click Attach Style Sheet from the CSS Styles panel (or use one of the nine zillion other ways to accomplish the same task, such as choose Attach Style Sheet from the Style list on the Property inspector), the Attach External Style Sheet dialog appears. Browse to or enter any CSS file and—before you click OK—choose Preview. Dreamweaver applies the selected style sheet and lists the new style sheet temporarily in the CSS Styles panel. Choose another CSS file and Preview is ready to give it another go. When you've found your heart's desire (in terms of style sheets, that is), choose Link or Import and then OK. Preview even works when one style sheet is already applied and you want to see what effect a new style sheet will have. Step lightly here, however: If your existing style sheet is selected in the CSS Styles panel, Dreamweaver imports or links your new sheet within the existing one. Although that could be the desired approach, often the goal is to include multiple style sheets in the main document. Click anywhere in the docu-ment to remove the highlight from a style sheet in the CSS Styles panel.

   CLICKABLE CELLS THAT CHANGE COLORS

This is another good one to keep handy in your Snippets panel—especially if you make it a habit to name classes the same way for all sites you develop. Have you ever wondered how to make a clickable cell that changes color when the users place their pointer over that cell? Here's what you do:

1. Make a custom class for the rollover effect. I've named mine .rollover.

2. Make a custom class for when the pointer isn't over the cell. I've named this custom class .plain.

3. Apply the .plain class to the `<td>` and then add the `onMouseOver` and `onMouseOut` events as shown in the code here, in the Behaviors panel.

   ```
   <td class="plain"
   onMouseOver="this.
   className='rollover';"
   onMouseOut="this.className=
   'plain';">
   ```

4. To make the cell clickable, select the `<td>` tag in the tag selector and then apply the Go To URL behavior in the Behaviors panel. Be sure the event is set as `onClick`.

5. For a final touch, add CSS to ensure the hand/pointer cursor is shown when users move their cursor over the cell as described in the Handy Pointer tip also in this chapter.

As you may have already guessed, this is one of those things that work in modern browsers only. For more compatibility with older browsers such as Netscape 4.x, make the text a hyperlink—depending on your preference—instead of or in addition to the Go To URL behavior.

    A SHORT COMMENTARY

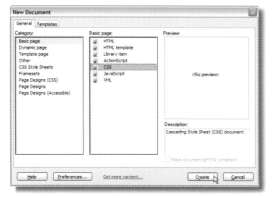

If you've chosen to create a CSS file from the New Document dialog box accessed from the File > New menu, you'll find that the file starts with a line like this:

```
/* CSS Document */
```

If you haven't guessed by now, that's a CSS comment. Althhough you can right-click (Ctrl+Click) and choose Selection > Comment Out Lines, the result is comments wrapped around each and every selected line individually which isn't nec-essary. You can avoid this by creating a snippet designed to wrap your current selection that uses `/*` for the Insert Before and `*/` for the Insert After fields. I like to add comments to my CSS file to help me remember how and why I used a particular definition. I even use CSS comments to remind myself of browser compatibility issues as shown in this example of a multi-line comment:

```
/*Application: <td> or <p> only
Browsers: IE 5+, NS 6+, Opera 5+ only. Netscape 4.x will not display the
border properly.
Notes: Be sure transparent images look okay against this dark background
color!*/
```

Your CSS files may get lengthy if filled with comments, but you can upload a copy without comments and keep the commented file for local use only. See the tip "/*Stripper*/" that teaches you how to remove comments using Find and Replace and regular expressions.

  HANDY DANDY TAG SELECTOR

That handy dandy tag selector in the lower left of the Document window even helps with custom classes. You may have noticed that if a tag already has a custom class applied the tag is shown with the custom class using dot notation like so: `<element.class>`. Similarly, if the tag has an ID already applied, it is represented in the tag

selector like so: `<element#id>`. So, if you have a paragraph with a custom class called .copyright, in the tag selector it looks like this: `<p.copyright>`. And if you have a `<div>` tag with the `ID` called content, it looks like this: `<div#content>`.

If you right-click (Ctrl+Click) a tag while in Design view, you will see the CSS Styles option. If you right-click a tag in the tag selector, you will see the Set Class option. In either of these submenus, you can apply a style if one hasn't been applied already, switch to a new style if a custom class has been applied (indicated by a checkmark), or choose None at the top of the list to remove the style already applied to the selected element.

   KING OF ALL MEDIA

Being the CSS jockey you are, you're probably aware that a style sheet can be targeted to specific media. One popular use of this feature is to include one style sheet for the screen and another for print. The W3C specifies nine different media attribute values, and these are at your fingertips in Dreamweaver. To specify a media type, link your page to an external style sheet, either via the CSS Styles panel by hand-coding. Then, place your cursor at the end of the `<link>` tag and press the spacebar; the CSS code hints display. Press M for media and then press Enter (Return) to confirm that choice. Presto—all nine media types are at your beck and call. Select any one from the hint list and crown yourself King of All Media. (Just don't tell Howard.)

```
 7  <link href="killerstyle.css" rel="stylesheet" type="text/css" media="p>
 8  </head>
 9
10  <body>
11  <h1> </h1>
12  <p>  </p>
13  </body>
14  </html>
15
```

all
aural
braille
handheld
print
projection
screen
tty
tv

   EXPORT CSS BIZ

Since I tend to hand-code most of my CSS, I like to create a document's initial CSS in the same document rather than in an external CSS file. Doing it this way saves me all the time spent toggling between the document I'm styling and the external CSS file. Once I get the CSS just right, I right-click (Ctrl+Click) inside the `<style>` block and choose CSS Styles> Export. Then I specify the CSS file that I want to use or type the name of a new one as prompted by the Export Styles As CSS File dialog box. Now I attach the CSS file by right-clicking (Ctrl+Clicking) in the `<style>` block and choosing CSS Styles > Manage Styles, and then I click the Attach button and complete the resulting dialog box. Finally, I manually delete the CSS from the document by first clicking the CSS icon in the Head Content bar. (Choose View > Head Content if you don't have it enabled already.) By now you may have noticed that I eliminated almost all need for the CSS Styles panel, which keeps my workflow moving along quickly.

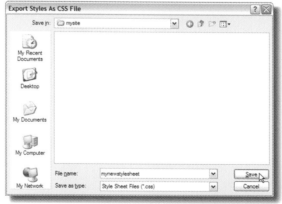

     CASE-BY-CASE CSS HIDING

If creating and maintaining a separate CSS style sheet just to make Netscape 4.x browsers happy seems like overkill to you, you're not alone. A growing number of developers are hiding rules from that browser on a case-by-case basis, all in one style sheet. The cool thing about this trick is that it has an added visual element to it, so the hidden styles are obvious even at a quick glance. Turns out that while all browsers ignore rules within a CSS-style comment (/*...*/), only Netscape 4.x continues to ignore those within a double or nested CSS comment. So this rule

```
#content {
font-size: 12px;
/*/*/
font-size: 100%;
/* */
}
```

displays the content text in Netscape 4.x at 12px, but sets the font size for more advanced browsers to 100% of the font size previously set in the body rule. (It's more common to write the comment indicators [the slashes and stars] inline with the rule, but I wanted to make it really obvious.) Talk about having your cake and eating it too!

     VERY !IMPORTANT

To help guarantee a style is given the highest priority you can take advantage of the keywords "!" and "important" following the property's value in the declaration. Let's say you have the following rule as part of your style sheet:

```
p{
color:#000000;
}
```

For whatever reason, the browser just isn't honoring this style. Try adding ! important following the property's value like so:

```
p{
color:#000000 !important;
}
```

Not only can you take advantage of ! important for use in browsers, but you can also use it in design time style sheets. (See "Design Time Style Sheets" also in this chapter for more information.)

    ## SWIMMING WITH THE CSS SHARKS

Thinking of dipping your foot in the CSS pool but afraid of getting bitten? Dreamweaver provides an easy way to set the basic overall CSS styles for your page. Select Modify > Page Properties, hit Ctrl-J (Command-J)—or use that new method noted in the "Page Property-Palooza" tip. No matter how you get there, once you open the Page Properties dialog, the Appearance category lets you easily establish simple CSS rules for the <body> modifying the general font face, size and color, as well as background color and/or image and margins. In the Links and Heading categories, you'll find similar contols for—yes, you guessed it—links and heading tags (<h1> through <h6>).

Setting CSS rules through the Page Properties dialog is strictly to get your feet wet though. The options are far more limited than what you'll find in either Dreamweaver's CSS Style Definition dialog or by hand-editing your style sheet. Moreover, the Page Properties dialog always inserts the CSS rules in the current document instead of using an external style sheet. (Of course, you can always follow the advice outlined in the "CSS Export Biz" tip found in this chapter to correct that.)

Oh, and by the way, there's at least one species of shark that loves CSS newbies: http://www.dwkillertips.com/go/19 is a great resource for Cascading Style Sheets.

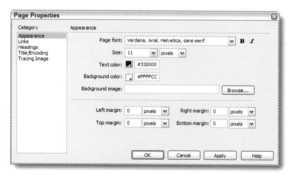

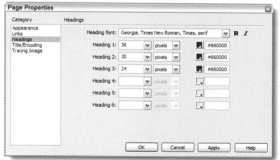

   FILTERED OR NON-FILTERED?

You can create the illusion of some cool effects without altering an image in an editor such as Fireworks. Mind you, this isn't for everyone—it is Internet Explorer proprietary. If that doesn't matter, however, you can have a load of fun. Check out the Filter drop-down list in the Extensions category of the CSS Style Definition dialog. You'll find an effect that turns a color image to black and white, an effect that makes an image look like an x-ray, and a whole lot more. You can use the filters on plain normal images, or for extra fun combine them with JavaScript. Here's an example of a CSS that uses the Invert effect when you place your pointer over an image that is a hyperlink:

```
.scary a:hover img {
filter: Invert;
}
```

Here's what the code might look like in the document:

```
<div id="Festival" class="scary">
<a href="festival.htm"><img src="festival.jpg" width="450" height="229"
border="0"></a>
</div>
```

Invert gives it a sort of creepy look, somewhat like a film negative. Remember that because these filters are proprietary, they won't validate as CSS. Because you are using a contextual selector, it must be entered in the New CSS Style dialog with the Use CSS Selector radio button chosen. Don't forget to apply the class to your HTML element, in this case that's a <div>.

Rapid Rows Cruising Columns

Header
Row
Ahead

Remember the first time you looked at the code for a complex table and tried to figure out why it was blowing up on one browser or another? Unless you're

Rapid Rows, Cruising Columns:
Building Better Tables

weirder than I am—and that's very weird— this is not like reminiscing about your first kiss. It's more like reliving the first fight you had where the school bully spun you over his head like a sack of lemons. (Don't tell me you've missed out on such a quintessential moment of growing up? If you think you have, it's only because you're in complete denial and require several years of regression thera- py to recover the memory.) Even if you're mov- ing away from tables as a layout tool, they remain an essential element of most every website for structured data and sliced graphics–and one that you need to master.

The tips in this chapter are designed to put you in the driver's seat when dealing with tables. The full gamut of table-related func- tionality is fair game here: structured data, formatted tables, layout tables, sliced graph- ics and more. You'll even find cool ways to work with data from Excel spreadsheets and Word tables. By the time you're finished with this chapter, you should have those tables spinning over your head like the proverbial fruit of your own choosing.

    HEIGHT DOESN'T MATTER

Many browsers don't recognize the height attribute in table code because it is deprecated. Stripping these attributes manually could take hours. A simple Find and Replace wouldn't work because the height values may differ, leaving you to double-check that all are removed. If you're going to run this on files that aren't open, be sure to make backups before you start, just in case.

Set up the Find and Replace dialog as shown in the figure accompanying this tip, but feel free to change the Find In option to suit your needs. Don't click Replace All just yet; you need to make sure that you only replace in `<table>`,`<tr>`,`<th>`, and `<td>`. Click Find All instead so that you can review the results first in the Results panel. You'll need to sort the results by clicking the Matched Text column header. If only the previously mentioned table tags are found, go ahead and click Replace All. If other tags are listed, such as the `<img>` tag, you'll want to replace one at a time, or jump on over to Chapter 10 to read "Replacing Within Results."

  ## QUICK COLUMN SELECT

To select an entire column in Dreamweaver, you used to need the motor skills of an Olympic gymnast. Placing your cursor in the 2-pixel zone on top of the column just so until the little arrow appeared and then clicking was always a, shall we say, challenge. Now, if you've got Table Widths enabled (View > View Options > Table Widths) or are in Expanded Table mode, you can just click any-where on the width indicator to select the column. You'll know you're in the right spot because all the column cells are highlighted, by default, with bright red lines. Click anywhere when you see the highlight, and your selection is complete. Now you can focus your motor skills on something more important, such as hitting the Mute button whenever a commercial comes on.

   ## UNDEFERRED, BUT NOT DETERRED

Long-time users of Dreamweaver who have never touched their Preferences might be a tad surprised the first time they work with a table in Dreamweaver MX 2004. Now, tables update automatically as you enter some text or other content—meaning the table cells adjust to reflect the amount of content added. In previous versions, an option in Preferences called Faster Table Editing (Deferred Updates) was checked by default. (Who's default it was, I'll never detail.) This option was originally put in the program because Dreamweaver's table-rendering speed was somewhat like that of a banana slug. Now, both Dreamweaver's routines and today's processors have quickened the pace quite a bit, making the option obsolete. Nonetheless, those folks who are not used to having their cells shoot around all over the place while they type might be in for a bit of a shock. The biggest adjustment I think is that sometimes the cells get too small before you can enter something in them to stretch 'em out again. This is particularly noticeable if you click from cell to cell. One solu-tion? Tab from one cell to the next: It will always get you into the cell you want to be in, and you can immediately type in any text you need or insert a graphic. Want another way to go? Switch into Expanded Tables Mode (F6) and your cells just got bigger and more accessible.

    PSEUDO-DECIMAL ALIGN

First day on the job and the boss asks whether I know Excel. Oh, sure, we're old pals. "Great, and I hear you know how to build webpages," he says. Yes, indeedy. "Excellent, well then, take this spreadsheet and bring it over to our site—and don't forget to line up all the decimal points." Uh…gulp. There is no decimal align in HTML, CSS, or any other web alphabet I know, so how am I going to pull this off?

Here are three techniques that will get your decimal ducks all in a row, assuming they all have the same number of digits to the right of the decimal point. Let's try the hard-core HTML version first. To begin, select and right-align the column with the decimals. This shoves those numbers right up against the cell wall—and it ain't a pretty sight. Next, position your cursor at the end of the first number and press Ctrl+Shift+Spacebar (Command+Shift+Spacebar) five or six times to put in a bunch of non-breaking spaces. You'll have to do that for all the numbers in the column (although you can copy and paste the spaces and I won't tell).

The second method is a bit more graphic, so close your eyes if you're squeamish. Instead of a series of non-breaking spaces, you place a transparent GIF image to the right. With the image selected, change the width in the Property inspector to 50 pixels or so. That moves those right-aligned numbers away from the border toot sweet. To do a bunch of cells in a column, Ctrl+Drag the resized image into place—that copies the graphic without having to go through a copy and paste.

Ready to go high tech? Here's the CSS code for doing the decimal shuffle:

```
.decimalAlign {
      text-align: right;
      padding-right: 100px;
}
```

Just select the whole column before you apply the style and you're good to go.

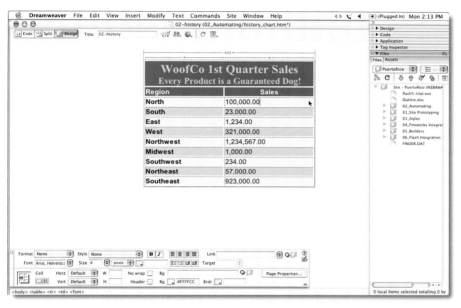

  CSS RENAMERONI

Ever run across a situation where you needed to rename a CSS style—but you'd already applied the style in a bunch of places and just couldn't face the agony of hunting them all down? Well, now you can rename the style without the agony. To rename a style, right-click (Ctrl+Click) the style in the CSS panel and, from the context menu, choose—you guessed it—Rename. If you're working with an internally defined style, Dreamweaver handles the renaming of both the style and all its applications with one small peep—a dialog box asking for the new name. If the style you're renaming is in an external style sheet, however, Dreamweaver asks whether you want to use Find and Replace to handle the renaming for you. Answer Yes and up pops the Find and Replace dialog with all the appropriate parameters—including the regular expressions required—to complete the rename. Choose Replace All (or do it on a case-by-case basis if you want with Replace Next), and before you're know it you're good to go. See, no agony, just ecstasy!

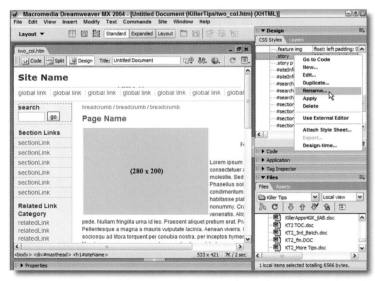

   KRAZY KUSTOM TABLE FORMATS

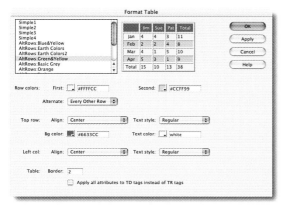

Talk about your thankless tasks rewarded. If you've have ever gotten stuck with the chore of reformatting a table full of data that hasn't been converted to CSS, you're going to love this tip. Dreamweaver includes a rather nifty tool found under Commands > Format Table. With it, you can quickly style a data table of any size.

Even though Format Table offers a lot of options—you can customize any of the 17 presets—the one thing it doesn't do is save your choices from session to session. Did you know that you can add your own custom format to the command? You have to pop the hood on the Dreamweaver JavaScript engine, but don't worry; it's basically a copy-and-paste job. To start, open the tableFormats.js file found in the Dreamweaver MX 2004\Configuration\Commands folder; this is where all the formats are stored. An entire format listing looks like this:

```
//Simple1
Formats[ ++i]  = new Array(); Formats[ i] .name="Simple1";
Formats[ i] .firstRowColor=""; Formats[ i] .secondRowColor="";
Formats[ i] .topRowTextStyle=BOLD; Formats[ i] .topRowAlign="";
Formats[ i] .topRowColor="#99FF00";
Formats[ i] .topRowTextColor="";
Formats[ i] .leftColTextStyle=ITALIC;
Formats[ i] .leftColAlign="";
Formats[ i] .border="0"; Formats[ i] .rowLimit="0";
```

Copy one entire format and paste it above the first format, Simple1—that makes your entry the first in the dialog. Now make any changes you want to any of the property values. Probably the first change you should make is the name; I named mine "Krazy Kustom" (don't ask). If you want to have alternating row colors, change the `rowLimit` value to anything other than zero—make it one to have every other row alternate or two for every two rows. For text styles (`topRowTextStyle` and `leftColTextStyle`), use one of four constants: `NONE`, `BOLD`, `ITALIC`, or `BOLD_ITALIC`.

For any other attribute, use an empty string (`" "`) to tell Dreamweaver not to assign a value. When you're done, save the JavaScript file and relaunch Dreamweaver. The next time you run the Format Tables command, you'll see your custom addition all nice and purty right there in the dialog—and you'll never have to customize again.

SPLITTING HAIRY ROWS

Nobody gets a table layout right the first time. Nobody. Seems like you always have to add a column or merge a row to get just the right setup. Suppose you've got a table with a single cell in the top row and six columns in the rest of the rows—and now you've got to split the top row into two equal cells. When you choose Split Cell from the Property inspector, Dreamweaver displays the dialog and suggests a number of columns to use, typically the maximum number of columns in the table. You might think, "Whoa, that's way more than I need; let me dial this puppy back a notch or two." But don't touch that dial! It's far better to initially split the cell into the maximum number of columns and then merge what cells are necessary to get the look you need. If you don't, you'll spend countless hours—okay, well maybe an extra 10 minutes or so—trying to get it right.

SORT AND FORMAT OR FORMAT AND SORT?

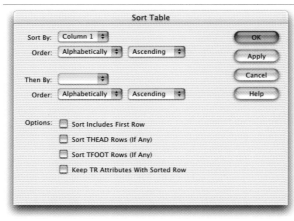

Sort Table and Format Table are real powerhouses when it comes to managing your tabular data; you'll find them both under the Commands menu. But if you need a formatted, sorted table, which command do you run first? And the answer is that word you love to hate, "depends." You can apply formatting to table elements two ways: the formatting attributes are either coded within each table row tag, <tr>, or within every table cell, <td>. If you would rather use the <tr> method, which offers cleaner code, format before you sort. On the other hand, if you want to go the <td> route for more granular control, sort first and format later. Opting for the second technique? Be sure to select the Apply All Attributes to TD Tags Instead of TR Tags option in the Format Table dialog box.

TABLE FORMATTING WITH CLASS

I advocate using CSS whenever possible for formatting, and that includes styling tables. You could use the Format Table command to get alternating row colors the way you'd like, but that adds so much more markup than if you were to just use CSS for styling. Trouble is, the Format Table command doesn't offer CSS as an option, and selecting every other row in Design view can be a tedious chore, prone to errors. Find and Replace to the rescue! First, make sure that you've removed any erroneous markup that will be defined in your CSS, then select the table you'd like to format in either Code or Design view. Then select Edit > Find and Replace and fill in the dialog accordingly:

Find in: Selected Text

Search: Source Code

Find: (<tr>([^>]*>[\S\s]*?</tr>[\S\s]*?<tr>([^>]*>[\S\s]*?</tr>)

Replace: $1 class="altRowColor1"$2 class="altRowColor2"$3

Options: Only Regular Expressions should be checked

Note that we have two custom classes, one named `altRowColor1` and the other `altRowColor2`. Feel free to use your own class names in their place; just be sure you've defined the classes in your CSS.

After you Replace All, look at the last `<tr>` in your table selection. If your selection had an odd number of rows, you must apply the class manually to this row.

To learn how alternate rows in ASP or ColdFusion, see Chapter 8's tip "Dynamic Alternations." If you're working in a template-based site, you also may consider looking in Chapter 6 at "Alternating Row Colors, The Template Parameter Way."

   AYE, AYE, CAPTION!

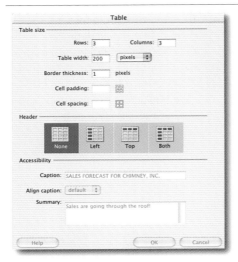

The move to create accessible websites has been extremely beneficial to a wide range of people. But even if you're not tasked with making your pages Section 508 compliant, you can spice up your tables—or at least make them more coherent—by using an accessibility oriented tag, `<caption>`. The `<caption>`... `</caption>` tag pair is typically placed just after the opening `<table>` tag; by default, the caption (whatever is enclosed by the `<caption>` tag) appears above the table, but you can display it underneath by changing the align attribute to bottom.

So what's the best way to add a caption to a table in Dreamweaver? The latest version of Dreamweaver brings the capability front-and-center: right in the ole Table dialog box. When you choose to insert a table, the Accessibility options are listed in their own section where you can enter your text in the Caption field and choose an alignment (top, bottom, left, or right). Coolness: You can edit the caption right in Design view if you need to make a change. If you're a hand-coder, go into Code view and drag and drop the Caption object from the Tables category of the Insert bar immediately following the opening `<table>` tag within the table structure. Then add your text and set the attributes by hand or use the Tag inspector with the `<caption>` tag selected.

   ## TABLE CENTERING IN THE HERE AND NOW

The center attribute for tables has gone the way of all deprecated tags—out the door into the cold. So, what's the best way to center your tables using CSS? To get the most coverage across browsers, you've got to take a two-class approach: one class to center align a `<div>` that goes around a table, and another to handle the table directly. The centered `<div>` CSS is pretty straightforward:

```
.centered {
text-align: center;
}
```

The table CSS is just a bit more elaborate:

```
.centered table{
text-align: left;
margin: auto;
}
```

By resetting the text-align attribute to left, all the table cells default to the left alignment; leave out this rule if you want your content in the tables to be centered as well. Now you're ready to be centered in the modern age.

   ## YOUR PAD IS MY SPACE; MY SPACE IS YOUR PAD

Do you ever find yourself unable to remember the simplest things? No? Okay, then skip this tip—you're obviously too good for it. For me, I can't seem to remember the difference between cell padding and cell spacing. One controls the number of pixels between cells, and one is the margin within the cells—but which is which?

By default, Dreamweaver leaves both these values blank when you first insert a table. Of course, not having a value doesn't mean the browser doesn't use any padding or spacing. Browsers display 2 pixels for both values if you don't specify a number. For a table full of structured data, I like to use rows with alternating background colors—which requires a 0 border and no room between the cells. (Otherwise, the background of the document will show through and break up the solid row background color.) Okay, so, in the Property inspector, I set the border to 0, but which of the two—cell padding or cell spacing—do I zero out? Here's my memory trick: I know I've got to set the Border to 0, and who is Border's good buddy, hanging out just to his left? Why it's old CellSpace! So, I set CellSpace to 0 also and I'm solid—and so is my background color.

  IT'S A WRAP!

When it comes to table cells, I'm not a big fan of letting my headers wrap from one line to another. Generally, a wrapped header in one cell tends to really throw off the design for all the others. However, I want to be sure that my content cells do wrap when needed. What's a poor, overworked web developer to do? Make those table header (`<th>`) tags wrapless! A little CSS in the right place is just the ticket. Include this rule:

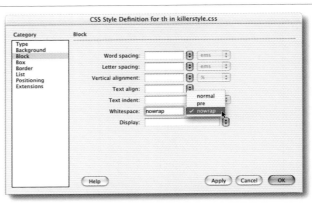

```
th {
white-space: nowrap;
}
```

And make sure your tables use `<th>` tags for all your header cells. You'll find the White-space option under the Block category for CSS attributes. Not only is it the proper thing to do, accessibility-wise, but your tables won't suffer the embarrassment of unwanted wrapping as my mother did whenever I whipped out my Eminem impression. (Whoops, wrong kind of rapping, g!)

   ACCESSIBLE STYLISH HEADERS

As mentioned in an the earlier tip ("Aye, Aye Caption!"), setting the Tables check box in the Accessibility category of Preferences brings up an additional dialog box when you are inserting a table. One of the options is to specify a header row, column, or both. Choose one of these selections and Dreamweaver converts the corresponding `<td>` tags to `<th>` tags. This action is taken to comply with §1194.22(g) of Section 508.

Browsers typically render `<th>` tags as bold and centered, which may or may not be the look you're going for. Using CSS, you can style the `<th>` tags however you like and still stay within compliance. Screen readers react to the tag itself, not the way that it is rendered.

IMPORTING STRUCTURED DATA: THE PREQUEL

Stuck in static land and can't go dynamic? Dreamweaver has a cool command that enables you to bring in data from a spreadsheet or database program—all you need to do is output the data in the proper format. And what's the proper format, you ask? Dreamweaver's File > Import > Tabular Data feature is pretty flexible and can work with almost any kind of text file where the data is separated or delimited by a certain character. Typically, you're trying to bring in data from either a spreadsheet program such as Microsoft Excel or a database pro- gram such as Microsoft Access. Just to mess with your head, these two programs use differ- ent commands to do the same thing. Here's a little help to get your data moving on the right track from those programs into Dreamweaver.

From Access, begin by selecting a table or query before choosing File > Export, and then set the Save As Type option to Text. Clear the Save Formatted check box. When you click Save, the Export Text Wizard appears. Although there are many ways to go, the best combo I've found is to choose Delimited on the first step and then select Comma as the delimiting character, with Quotes as the Text Qualifier. (If your data has quotation marks in it, choose Tab as a delimiter and None as the Text Qualifier.)

From Excel, select File > Save As and choose either Text (tab-delimited) or CSV (comma- delimited). Again, the decision depends on what's in your data—for the most part, I go with the tab-delimited files. Whichever you choose, make sure that Dreamweaver is set to use the corresponding delimiter in the Import Tabular Data dialog, or you're in for a heap of cleanup.

LEAVING THE NEST

Ever get so deep into nested tables you can't see straight? Dreamweaver offers a way to clear up that double (or triple) vision. If you're in Layout view, you can unnest a table with one click o' the button. Just select the table you want to throw out of the nest and click Remove Nesting from the Property inspector—the same command is available from the context menu of a selected nested table.

TABLE WIDTHS ON A NEED TO KNOW BASIS

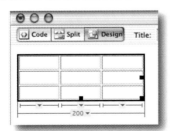

The first time you insert a table, Dreamweaver displays a preset width value of 75%; you also can set the width in pixels if you prefer. What many people don't grasp is that you don't have to declare a table width at all, and in many cases it is better not to. Don't misunderstand me; I'm not advocating that you eliminate the width value when you create your table—if you do that, you'll get an impossibly skinny table that you're going to have to expand to insert your content. No, the way to do it is to keep the table at whatever width you are comfortable with as you add your text, images, and what-have-you. When you're done, select the Clear Column Widths button on the Table Property inspector (it's the top left in the group of six buttons). Now the information is free to flow and the table cells will be only as wide as the content needs them to be.

68   CHAPTER 3 · Building Better Tables

  ## MAINTAIN COLUMN WIDTHS

There's nothing special about dragging a cell's border to adjust its width. The table's width stays the same, and all column widths change. It used to be that when I wanted a table to change width, I'd have to carefully drag the table border and then make adjustments to column widths individually. Now you can do both in just one step. If you hold the Shift key down while dragging a cell's border, the other column widths remain their original size and just the selected column's width and the table's width change. While you have the key pressed, and when you start to drag, you'll even see some handy lines that indicate the placement of the adjusted columns.

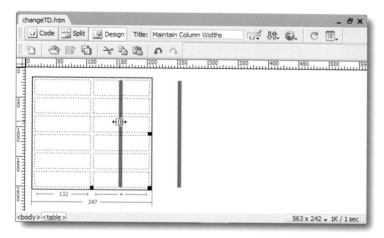

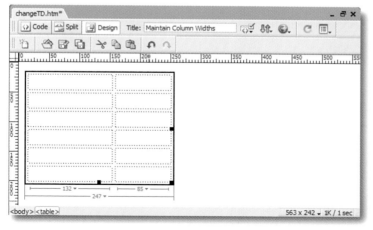

MOVING CELLS AND CELL CONTENTS

Got some cellular matter to relocate? You can move entire rows or columns simply by cutting and pasting. Rows will appear above the current cursor position and columns will appear to the left. So how do you move a row or column to the outside? Add a temporary column or row by increasing the number of columns or rows in the Table Property inspector. Then, place your cursor in the newly created column or row and paste away. The content shows up next to the cursor, and now you're free to delete your temporary column or row.

THIS TIP TOTALLY RULES

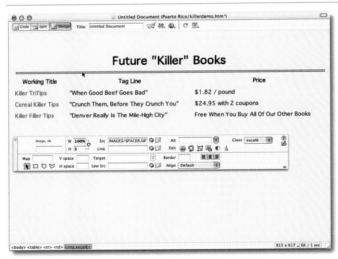

Sometimes it is helpful to separate multiple-column content in the same table with a straight line or rule. I can think of a couple of ways to fulfill this wish right off the bat. Generally, I start by making sure that the content rows I want to separate have at least one row between them—call this the rule row. Select the rule row and merge all the cells into one. Now you have the choice of inserting a horizontal rule tag, `<hr>`, or a small colored GIF (like 2 pixels x 2 pixels). Change the width of either to 100% and, as they say in pseudo-France, woilah.

   ## BATTLE OF THE IRON DESIGNERS

So, you want to challenge the Iron Designer of NY, eh? You select a table with a mouse and I'll do the same with the keyboard. Ready? Go! Beat 'cha…. How'd I do it? The same keyboard shortcut usually used for selecting everything on the page—Ctrl+A (Command+A)—works differently within a table. The first time you press it, the table cell is selected; the second time, the entire table is highlighted. How fast can you press the same keyboard combination twice in a row? Pretty fast, right? Actually this shortcut walks up the table structure, so it's even more valuable when working with nested tables. In other words, first the <td> is selected, and then the <table> that holds the <td>; if that <table> is nested (and therefore also in a <td>), the next time you press Ctrl+A/Command+A, the outer table is selected.

Want to go again? Okay, this time let's add a row. Ready? G … I'm done. That's just how quickly I can press Ctrl+M (Command+M), which inserts a new row above the cursor. Best two out three? How about deleting a row? Whoa—almost got me that time, but only because I had to do a Ctrl+Shift+M (Command+Shift+M). There are equivalent keyboard shortcuts for adding a column—Ctrl+Shift+A (Command+Shift+A)—and deleting one— Ctrl+Shift+Minus (Command+Shift+Minus). By the way, make sure you're in Standard or Expanded Table mode when you hold this little contest—the shortcuts don't work in Layout mode and you'll be left holding the proverbial bag.

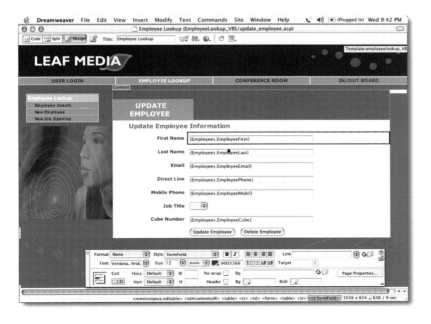

   ## BATTEN DOWN THE (TABLE) HATCHES

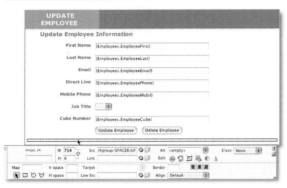

Watch out, there's a big storm of nasty browsers heading your way. If your table structure is not locked down tight, they might blow it out of the water. Some of the earlier browsers had a bad habit of adjusting cell widths and heights willy-nilly; if you've ever seen an exploded table, you know it's not a pretty sight. What's a poor table builder supposed to do?

Let's borrow a technique from our brethren in the web tool biz, the graphic editors. When you slice up an image in a program such as Fireworks or Photoshop and export it, the graphic becomes a table of images. Holding the table tightly together is an additional row and another column, filled with a transparent single-pixel GIF image. The GIFs, often called a shim or spacer when it is used like this, are set to a specific width across the top of the table, corresponding to the column width; the same method sets the height of the spacer to the row heights. (You don't actually change the size of the file or the image, just the width and height in the <img> tag.) Together the added row and column make it impossible to break apart the table structure. So where do you get these marvelous wee beasties? If you've imported any sliced graphics into your site, you probably already have them.

   ## BRINGING IN THE SHIMS

If you started looking around for a transparent GIF image after reading the "Batten Down the (Table) Hatches" tip, you don't need to look very far. Dreamweaver has the capacity to add a shim row to any column in any table—the feature is built into Layout mode. When you're in Layout mode, select the width indicator for a given column and choose Add Spacer Image. If you don't have a spacer image set for the current site yet, Dreamweaver will either let you pick one or create one for you—which you can store wherever you want. All succeeding spacers use the same GIF, so there's no chance of a bunch of little files overtaking your site.

THE VAST EMPTINESS OF WAY OUT, LAYOUT SPACE

Looking at your tables in both Standard and Layout view is free and easy. But suppose that you want to add some content to the table while in Layout view—now that's gonna cost you some energy units. Okay, the tariff isn't that high—any cells with content already in them can be added to or modified at no extra charge. Totally empty cells or cells with just a nonbreaking space in them, however, well, that's another matter. Layout view sees such blank cells as just structural and not load bearing, if you will. To insert text, graphics, or any other content into an empty cell in Layout view, you need to explicitly draw the cell. Dreamweaver helps by snapping to the edges of existing cells, but you still need to push that mouse around to make it happen.

SNAP GOES THE MOUSE

Drawing cells and tables in Layout view is quite literally a snap. To make it easy to create coherent structures, Dreamweaver defaults to snapping new cell and table borders to those already on the page. Just get within eight pixels of an existing edge and—*snap!*—you're locked into position. That's all well and good for most designs, but suppose that you want to draw out a cell not exactly touching its neighbor? To temporarily override the snapping border, hold down the Alt (Option) key while drawing a layout cell. To contemporaneously ride a snapping turtle—you're on your own.

   # C(LA)SS-IC FLUID AND SET COLUMNS

Let's take a look at another way to create a combo fluid and set column layout, this time with CSS. There are a lot of variations you can start with, but let's keep it basic. This tasty recipe calls for three CSS definitions, one for the fixed width column, one for the fluid column, and a third one to contain them both:

```
#sidebar{
        float : left;
        width : 190px;
        background-color: #FFFF66;
}
#content{
        margin: 0 auto 0 200px;
        position: relative;
        background-color: #CCFFFF;
}
#container{
    width: 100%
}
```

The #sidebar rule, applied to a <div> tag containing the navigation, is set to a fixed 190 pixels and floated to the left. The #content rule—set to the content <div> of course— uses a margin setting that starts the left margin at 200px (10 pixels away from the sidebar) and allows the right margin to move "auto" magically; it's important that a relative position is used as well. The final rule, #container, spans the whole page with a 100% width and is applied to a <div> tag that encompasses the other two <div> tags.

There are the bare-bones rules; you should add padding and other attributes to taste (I added a bit of color to make the differences noticeable). I like to use the Div Tag feature from the Insert bar's Layout Category to create the necessary tags and instantly apply the appropriate CSS by selecting the desired ID. When you're done, your layout should flow like the proverbial wind.

74 CHAPTER 3 · Building Better Tables

CALLING ALL BORDERS

Creating a bordered text box in CSS is pretty easy, but if you can't use CSS on your site (sob!), there's a way to get the same effect with tables (yay!). The trick is to nest one table inside another where the outer table has both a background color (that becomes your border) and a small amount of cell padding (which translates into the border width). The inner table is set to 100% width, a larger cell padding value, to keep it away from the outer border, and given its own background color. The interesting thing about using this technique to create a border is that no border attributes are used—or rather, they are specifically not used and set to 0—for both tables. Here's some sample code to gnaw on:

```
<table width="250" border="0" cellpadding="1"
cellspacing="0"
bgcolor="#000000" >
<tr>
<td> <table width="100%" border="0" cellspacing="0"
cellpadding="20"bgcolor="white">
<tr>
<td bgcolor="#FFFF99" align="left" valign="top">
<h3 align="center">Crossing The Border</h3>
<p>Cross-browser bordered tables are highly legal.</p>
</td>
</tr>
</table>
</td>
</tr>
</table>
```

Blazing Browsers

Real World Browser Techniques

We all know what a drag it is to make pages that look good in older browsers like Netscape 4.x. To make your site look the same in older browsers and modern

Blazing Browsers:
Real World Browser Techniques

ones, you often must sacrifice the appearance of the site. Bear in mind that it is rare that someone—other than web developers or clients—will see your page in both older and newer browsers. Typically, the general public uses only one browser or another and will never compare a site between browsers. All that really matters is that the site looks acceptable and is fully functional in the browsers of your target audience. Read the last few sentences over and over again until you've committed them to memory. You'll be better for it, and you won't consider wasting precious time making every last detail the same between browsers.

Everything you'll find in this chapter relates to browsers in some way, shape, or form. Not only do you learn cool tips for Dreamweaver, but you also learn general browser usage tips that will speed up work-flow and make you a better all-around developer. You'll get solutions to tough issues specific to certain browsers, fun things you can do for some browsers, and a bunch of ideas you never considered before.

   BYE BYE RESIZE FIX

For many developers, long gone are the days of supporting Netscape 4.x browsers. If you're among this group, you want to be sure that Dreamweaver no longer adds the Netscape Resize Fix to your pages automatically. Select Edit > Preferences (Dreamweaver > Preferences), and then choose the Layers category on the left. Uncheck the Netscape 4 Compatibility box, and then click OK. If you happen to want the fix, you can add it to your documents on a case-by-case basis using Commands > Add/Remove Netscape Resize Fix.

   CLOSE POP-UP WINDOW

What do you do if you want to give users a way to close a pop-up window that they're viewing? Provide a close link, of course. Just select the text or image that you want to use as a link, and then in the Link field of the Property inspector enter the following code: `javascript:self.close();`. Want the window to close automatically if the user leaves the page without closing it? Add the script to an `onBlur` event in the `<body>` tag!

As if that isn't easy enough, there's a free extension, DWfaq Close Pop-up Window, which you can apply from the Behaviors panel. You can find the extension at http://www.dwkillertips.com/go/20.

 BROWSER SUICIDE

You've already learned how to close a pop-up window in the "Close Pop-Up Window" tip on the previous page. Did you try it on a parent window—a window that isn't a pop-up window? If you try that method, you will get a browser security warning. The warning dialog definitely sounds scary to the average website viewer.

So how do you kill the parent window? Ask most anyone and she'll tell you it can't be done because it is a security issue. She might suggest an ActiveX control, but many users disallow those. In fact, if this tip doesn't work for you, it means that the browser makers have gotten wise to this technique and have patched this security hole.

The JavaScript is so darn simple, you might even smack your forehead and say, "Why didn't I think of this?" I sure did when I first learned of this code.

```
function suicide(){
self.opener = self;
self.close();
}
```

Call the function from an event on the `<body>` tag or a hyperlink. For example:

```
<a href="javascript:;" onClick="suicide()">Kill me!</a>
```

I don't suspect that this function will work forever in all browsers. They're bound to catch on sooner or later. In the meantime, enjoy this one and use it to wow your geek friends. Just please don't use it for evil!

   <HEAD> 'EM OFF

Dreamweaver includes a pretty flexible behavior called Check Browser that stays on the current page or redirects the user to a different page, depending on the browser version. When you apply the Check Browser behavior, it is triggered by the `onLoad` event of the `<body>` tag; in other words, after the page has finished loading, the JavaScript code checks the browser and redirects the page according to your settings. This is all well and good if one of your options is to stay on the same page—but what if you've got two separate pages you're redirecting to? With the standard Dreamweaver implementation, the page has to load before it redirects; even if the page is blank, you may get a little flash of the page before the redirection kicks in. The way around this is to move the function call that Dreamweaver inserted in the `<body>` tag up to the `<head>`. To do this, locate the `onLoad` event in the `<body>` tag; it'll look something like this:

```
<body
onLoad="MM_checkBrowser(4.0,1,2,4.0,0,2,2,'main.htm','altmain.htm');
return document.MM_returnValue">
```

Copy the bolded code from your own `<body>` tag and paste it within the `<script>` tag in the `<head>`, just above the line that starts with function `MM_checkBrowser`. You also need to delete the entire `onLoad` event in the `<body>` tag. Now, just like with a server-side redirection script, the redirection takes place in the blink of an eye—without the flash of a page.

Check Browser		
Netscape Navigator: 4.0 or later,	Go to URL	OK
otherwise,	Go to alt URL	Cancel
Internet explorer: 4.0 or later,	Stay on this page / Go to URL / ✓ Go to alt URL	Help
otherwise,		
Other browsers	Go to alt URL	
URL: home.html		Browse...
Alt URL: losers.html		Browse...

   NOT YOUR ONLY FTP

If you're like me, and have been using Dreamweaver's FTP and no other dedicated FTP program in your workflow, you may find yourself stuck waiting for Dreamweaver to finish uploading or downloading files before you can get back to work. Occasionally Dreamweaver chokes on extra-large files, leaving you no choice but to find another way to upload/download files. Usually when I upload or download a file, it is the perfect time to check email, or grab a snack. At other times, however, I have a lot to do and just don't want to wait.

What many of us Windows users seem to forget is that we already have other FTP-enabled software installed—software that we use every day—our browsers! That's right; you can use Internet Explorer or Netscape to access your site's files. The usual formula is ftp://www.dwkillertips.com , where www.dwkillertips.com is either your domain or IP address. The user is then prompted with a dialog for username and password. But wait, there's more: ftp://username:password@dwkillertips.com is the formula to bypass that dialog. Just replace username:password@ with the account's username followed by a colon and then the account password, followed by the @ symbol and then the domain.

This is also handy for providing FTP access to clients who aren't `<gasp/>` using Dreamweaver. To make it completely foolproof, you can tack on the directory path at the end like a normal hyperlink, putting your client in exactly the right directory.

   JOINING THE <A> TEAM

Dreamweaver newbies applying their first behavior are faced with a mind-twisting choice—make the wrong move and you're cutting off your browser backward compatibility. For example, suppose that you're applying a Show-Hide Layer behavior to an image and you want the behavior to fire when the user rolls over an image—so you pick **onMouseOver** from the Events listing, right? But what about that other choice: **<A> onMouseOver**) ? What's the difference and what's the best choice? You'll see both sets of choices when your Show Event For options includes any of the Internet Explorer 4.0–6.0 or Netscape 6.0 browsers.

Choose the event without the **<A>** and the behavior is applied to the $<img>$ tag itself. That's okay—if you don't care about your rollover working in Netscape 4.x browsers. Select the event with the **<A>**, however, and you're covered all the way; the behavior is applied to an automatically added $<a>$ tag, and that works in all fourth-generation browsers and above.

   ALRIGHT, NETSCAPE 4.X, HOLD THOSE MARGINS, BUDDY!

So, you're cool, you're hip, you're savvy—you nod knowingly when fellow web designers mention the "@ Import trick" (if you don't, sneak over to Chapter 2, quick like a bunny)—but what do you put in those style sheets intended for only Netscape 4.x? One of the headache-inducing Netscape 4.x issues is how it handles page margins. With Internet Explorer 4+ or Netscape 6 and greater, use CSS to set the $<body>$ margins to 0 and you're done; with earlier versions of Netscape, it's hoop-jumping time. First, in the Netscape-specific style sheet— the one you link, not import—set the top and left margins to –10. Yes, that's negative 10. Why? Don't ask. Next, in the Page Properties dialog (Modify > Page Properties), set Margin Width and Margin Height both to 0. (One caveat: Right and bottom margins are supported by Netscape 4, so this tip won't help table layouts set to 100%.) With both the CSS and HTML specifications in place, Netscape 4.x margins are as snug as a bug in a rug.

BROWSER CHECKING WITHOUT THE BROWSER

There's what, a gazillion browser versions in use on the web now? Oh, wait, I forgot about the latest release—make that a gazillion and one. How do you check your pages against them all when you can't possibly have all the browsers? Dreamweaver's Target Browser Check is one often-overlooked alternative that gives you a way to check your entire site against 16 major browser versions. To see the possibilities, choose Window > Results, then click the Target Browser Check tab, and then select the green arrow to get started. Selecting all the browser versions in the Target Browser Check will definitely lead you to say, "Well, you can't please all the people all the time," unless your page is just bare text. It's best to decide which browsers you intend to support and just run Target Browser Check against them. I, for example, rarely check for anything below a version 4 browser these days—it all depends on the client's web statistics. If the logs show that 15% of the site's visitors are using Netscape 2.0, I'm going to be sure the site looks acceptable in that browser.

CONDITIONAL COMMENTS

It's just a fact of life that not all browsers render code the same way. Even browsers of the same brand but varying versions can cause issues. That's one reason why there are so many different "browser sniffer" scripts available on the web. After the browser is determined, rendering variations may be accounted for using JavaScript or the users may be redirected to a page specifically for their browser. If all you're interested in is changing something specifically for Internet Explorer, you'll find that conditional comments are a much simpler way to go. Conditional comments are only recognized in Internet Explorer 4 and above, whereas non-Internet Explorer browsers treat them as regular HTML comments that are not seen by the browser. You can put virtually anything you want between the opening and ending conditional comment syntax. The syntax is simple; if less than Internet Explorer, do all this stuff until you get to the endif syntax.

```
<!--[ if lt IE 6]>
Please upgrade to Internet Explorer 6.
<![ endif] -->
```

As you may have guessed, you can check for other browser versions, and use operators such as gt for greater than, gte for greater than or equal to, and several other operators. I'd better just show you where to find the rest of the operators; all you need to know about conditional comments, you can find at the MSDN site: http://www.dwkillertips.com/go/21.

  PLACEMENT, PLACEMENT, PLACEMENT

If you've ever looked at a layer-based page in a browser that is not layer capable, you know that you can get into a big mess in a big hurry. There is, however, a technique that gives you the best possible solution for both layer and nonlayer browser worlds—and that's placement. The earlier browsers don't understand the `<div>` tag and so it's totally ignored; as I'm sure you know, `<div>` tags are used by Dreamweaver to create layers by

default. They do, however, understand and render the content within those tags. It's good practice to place your `<div>` tags in the HTML document in the order in which they should appear: For example, the heading area should go above the content, which should, in turn, go above the footer. Dreamweaver inserts the code, depending on the cursor placement. How do you re-order your `<div>` tags? Although you could cut and paste the code, I prefer to drag the layer icons into place. If you don't see the little yellow icons for layers, you will need to make sure that the Anchor Points for Layers is checked in the Invisible Elements section of Edit > Preferences (Dreamweaver > Preferences) and that View > Visual Aids > Invisible Elements is enabled.

   PREVIEWING ROOT-RELATIVE LINKS LOCALLY

Did you know that Dreamweaver manages a little slight of hand that makes it possible to preview pages with site-root-relative links (up to a point, anyway)? As I'm sure you know, document-relative links preview just fine in Dreamweaver. Dreamweaver creates the temporary file it actually sends to the browser in the same folder as the current page being previewed—so, document-relative links are a snap. Site-root-relative links are a different story, however. Let's say that you're working on a page that is saved in a folder three levels deep in your site and you have an `<img>` tag with a `src` set to `/assets/images/logo.gif`. How does Dreamweaver's Preview in Browser (which is just working with the local file system, not an actual HTTP-type URL) know where to get the image? If you look at the source when previewing, you'll see that Dreamweaver actually converts the site-root-relative link to a document-relative one. This means that the image `src` in this example would become `../../assets/images/logo.gif`. This works swell for the first page, but if you want to check links from that page, you're better off previewing through a server—either locally or remotely. Why? Dreamweaver's bit of legerdemain extends only to the first page previewed; any site-root-relative links on a second page go untranslated.

THE LAYER LOW-DOWN

Ready to make the move from table-based layout to CSS-P and looking for a leg up? Dreamweaver's Modify > Convert > Tables to Layers might seem like a quick fix, but it's a pretty sharp double-edged sword. The command is pretty thorough; if anything, it's a little too thorough. Every object in the `<body>`, regardless of whether it is in a table, gets placed into a layer. How about example of such pedal-to-the-metal efficiency? Every content-filled (or background-using) cell within a table is put into a separate layer. For example, if you convert a page with a 3×5 table, you'll end up with 15 layers. Bottom line: Use Convert Tables to Layers judiciously.

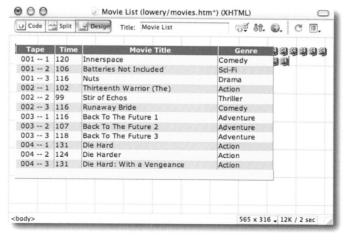

   NOT AN IFRAME

I've personally found no practical use for this trick; other people seem to like it, however, so I'll share it with you too. The illusion of an iFrame can be created in Internet Explorer with a simple bit of CSS that looks something like this:

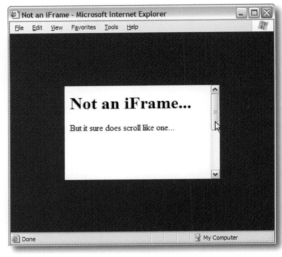

```
html{
border: #333333 100px solid;
}
```

Create a new style in Dreamweaver by clicking the New CSS Style icon in the lower portion of the CSS panel. Make sure that the radio is set to Selector Type: Tag. Enter or select HTML in the Tag field. Choose whether you want the code in the current document only or in an external CSS file, and then click OK. Move to the Borders category in the CSS Style Definition for HTML dialog and select your border options. When done, click OK. Then preview the results in Internet Explorer. You'll see that the browser scrollbar is pulled into the page creating the illusion of an iFrame.

   QUIT MAKING ME QUIRKY!

You're familiar with doctype switching, right? This is the way that modern browsers (i.e., Internet Explorer and Netscape version 6 and later browsers as well as Safari) render the page in a strict standards-based compliance mode or in a looser, so-called quirks mode, depending on the document type declared. Seems like there's another wrinkle for those designers creating XHTML-compliant pages. In the previous version Dreamweaver included the XML encoding declaration at the top of every XHTML page. Unfortunately, this threw Internet Explorer 6 into quirks mode, which causes the page to render differently than it should. You'll be happy to know that with Dreamweaver MX 2004, you no longer have a to worry about XML encoding declarations hanging over your `<head>`—they are no longer automatically inserted. (And for those dealing with legacy pages, there's a pot of gold waiting for you at DreamweaverFAQ.com. Co-author Angela Buraglia has developed an extension called Strip `<? xml?>` Tag that zaps that quirk-causing code automatically. It works for HTML and PHP files but magically leaves XML files untouched—best of all, it's free! Go grab yourself some gold at http://www.dwkillertips.com/go/22.)

WHAT'S UP, DOCTYPE?

Dreamweaver MX 2004 is way better about validating webpages. But there are a bunch of standards out there—how does Dreamweaver know which standard to measure the file against? Just like a validation service, it looks first to see if the file has a declared DOC-TYPE—and if so, it uses that DOCTYPE as the measuring stick. But what if there is no DOCTYPE declared? A whole lot of legacy Dreamweaver documents fall into that category because until recently, the default file was created without a DOCTYPE. In these circumstances, Dreamweaver uses whatever is declared in the Validator category of Edit > Preferences (Dreamweaver > Preferences).

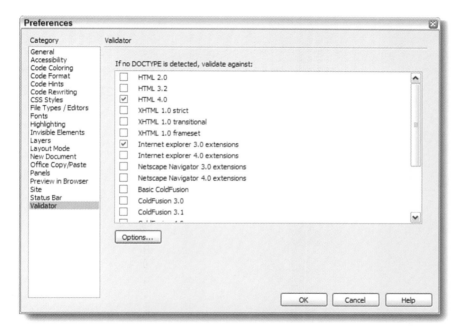

   SASSY STATUS BAR

Way down at the bottom of the browser window lives the status bar. Usually, the status bar provides helpful info, such as the progress of the loading page or the URL of the hyperlink the pointer is over. My favorite use of the status bar is to provide a copyright message when the user's pointer is over an image. Sometimes I use the status bar for a description of the image. Dreamweaver makes doing status bar messages easy with the Set Text of Status Bar behavior. First, make the image a link, be it real or null (see "Watch Out for Killer Octothorpes" in Chapter 7), and then click the Add (+) button on the Behaviors panel and choose Set Text > Set Text of Status Bar. When the dialog appears, type **You Taka My Stuff, I Breaka You Face** or another appropriate message, and then click OK. Make sure that you've chosen the appropriate event in the Behaviors panel. In our case, we want **<A> onMouseOver** so that the behavior is applied to an <a> tag that wraps the <img> tag. (Dreamweaver adds the <a> tag if it doesn't already exist.) If you want the message to disappear when the pointer moves off the image, apply the behavior a second time, but don't add a message—just click OK and leave the dialog blank. Don't forget to set the event to **<A> onMouseOut**. Make sure to preview so that you're certain all of your text appears in the status bar as intended; you're limited to the number of characters that fit the width of the given browser.

     ## SNAPPY BROWSER SIZING

It sure is handy to have the ability to resize a browser window when you are doing site testing. Just a simple snippet of JavaScript can resize most any browser window. The `resizeTo()` function lets you specify a width and height argument that will snap the current browser window to the specified width and height values. Let's create a page in Dreamweaver that you will view in the browser to later make into a browser "Favorite" or "Bookmark". Click the Hyperlink object found in the Common category of the Insert bar. In the Text field, enter the text you want your Favorites/Bookmarks to display. I've used Resize to 800x600. In the Link field, type **javascript:resizeTo(800,600)**, and then click OK. Now view the page in a browser. Right-click (Ctrl+Click) the hyperlink and select either Add to Favorites or Add Bookmark (or a similar command) from the context menu. If you are prompted that what you are adding may not be safe, confirm that it is okay to add it. Some browsers even let you click and drag the link into the browser toolbar so that the function is available as a button. Now whenever you want to resize a browser, just choose the favorite you created. To make your life easier, I've put together a few for you here: http://www.dwkillertips.com/go/23.

   ELIMINATE THE INTERNET EXPLORER 6 IMAGE TOOLBAR

Surf the Internet using Internet Explorer 6 and
sooner or later you'll get a glimpse of the Image
toolbar. Usually an image that is equal to or more
than 200px by 200px is required to make the
Image toolbar appear, but there are other factors
that can allow for it to be shown on images as
small as 124px by 124px. I try not to worry about
what will or will not make the Image toolbar
appear and just add the `<meta>` tag needed to
turn it off. In the Head menu, in the HTML category of the Insert bar, click the Meta object. Select
the HTTP-equivalent option from the Attributes
drop-down list, type `<meta>` in the Value field, type **no** in the Content field, and then click
OK. The inserted `meta` tag in the Head of your page should say `<meta http-
equiv="imagetoolbar" content="no">`. You also can handle the Image toolbar on a
case-by-case basis by adding a `galleryimg` attribute to the `<img>` tag with a value of `no`,
using the Properties section of the Tag inspector or via Code view.

   MULTIPLE PREVIEW

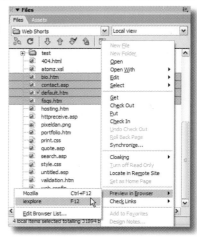

Many times I've needed to work with multiple files and
preview them in the browser. So I open them all up and
then one by one I press F12 to view them. This was a
major "Duh!" moment when I realized that I can preview them all in one shot. In the Files panel, Ctrl+Click
(Command+Click) each file you need to preview or
click once and then Shift+Click a few files away to get
all files between the first and second click. Use the
Preview in Browser keyboard shortcut F12 (primary
browser) or Shift+F12 (secondary browser) or right-
click (Ctrl+Click) the selection in the Files panel and
choose your browser from the Preview in Browser submenu. All the pages will either open in the same window, so that you can use your browser's Back button to
navigate between pages, or they'll open in their own
browser windows, for you to view, and close, at your leisure. This behavior is dependent
upon browser versions, what OS you're running, and what your preferences in some
browsers are set to.

     EDIT BROWSER LIST

Previewing pages early and often in various browsers will save you on the cost of headache medicine. To make this agonizing process a bit less painful, set up additional browsers for Dreamweaver to use with its Preview in Browser feature. Select Edit > Preferences (Dreamweaver > Preferences) or Ctrl+U (Command+U), and then click Preview in Browser from the Category list on the left. Don't give the browser a name just yet, or when you do the next step the value in the Name field will be replaced. Now click the Add (+) button and browse to the executable file for your installed browser. Next, give the browser a meaning-ful friendly name. This is the name that will appear in the menu. Finally, decide if you want this to be the primary browser that is accessed by the keyboard shortcut F12 or the second-ary browser accessed by Shift+F12 or neither. You don't have to make it primary or second-ary, if you'd rather access the browser from the menu File > Preview in Browser submenu. By the way, Windows users, you can install as many Netscape browsers as your machine can tolerate but only one Internet Explorer.

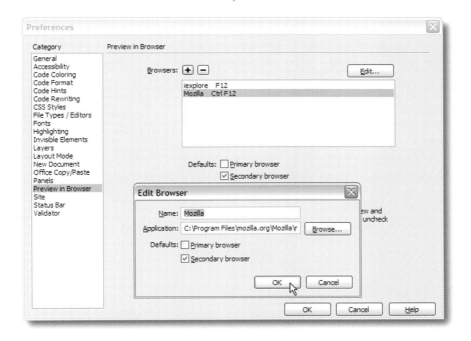

   INTERNET EXPLORER QUICK SCROLL

Scrolling down a seemingly endless page is never any fun. This little tip might save you some sanity, although I'm sure it is debatable. Right-click the scrollbar of a lengthy page in Internet Explorer (Windows only) and you'll get a handy little context menu that lists several helpful scrolling options. What can I say? I just love context menus.

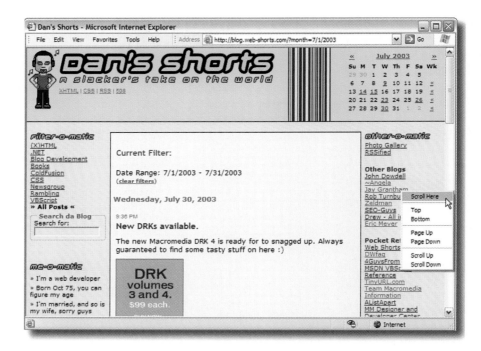

    MAKE DREAMWEAVER THE DEFAULT EDITOR

One of the best ways to learn is to examine existing pages on the web. Internet Explorer offers an Edit button on its toolbar that will open the current page in the editor selected. I've tested out this tip in IE 5.5 on Windows 2000 and IE 6 on Windows XP. If you're using another Windows operating system or Internet Explorer version, this may or may not work. That said, let's make Dreamweaver available as the default editor for Internet Explorer. First you need to open any folder on your system in Windows Explorer, and then choose Tools > Folder Options. Click the File Types tab, and then select HTML from the list of Registered File Types. Now click the Advanced button. Click Edit in the list of Actions, and then click the Edit button. In the Application used to perform action field, browse the Dreamweaver MX 2004 executable file. Whatever appears in that field must include quotations around the path, followed by a space, and then %1, so that it looks something like this:

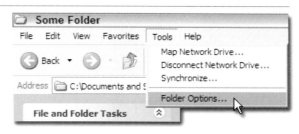

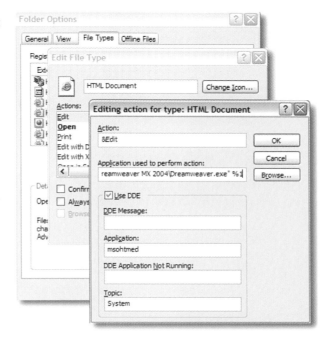

```
"C:\Program Files\Macromedia\Dreamweaver MX 2004\Dreamweaver.exe" %1
```

Now launch Internet Explorer if it isn't open already, and choose Tools > Internet Options and select the Programs tab. Assuming that all went well in the previous steps, you should be able to select Dreamweaver MX 2004 from the HTML editor drop-down list and click OK. Now the Edit button on the toolbar should open the current page in Dreamweaver MX 2004 so that you can examine or edit the code.

   HIDE FOCUS

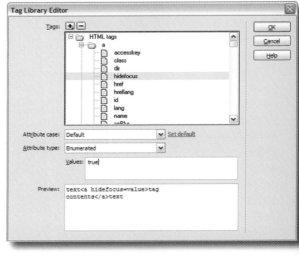

Ask your web developer friends how to remove those dotted lines around images, hyperlinks, and form buttons, and they'll probably give you a snippet of JavaScript to do the job. The focus lines are there as a browser accessibility feature, but there may be instances where the lines are undesirable. Instead of relying on JavaScript to do the job, you can use a little-known attribute supported in Internet Explorer 5.5 and higher only. You can add `hidefocus="true"` to `<a>`, `<input>`, or `<img>` tags. The `<area>` tag is supposed to be supported, but it really isn't—at least not in all my extensive testing. I did find that if you add the attribute to the `<img>` tag, that will work on image maps (`<area>` tags). A slight disadvantage

to this method is that it is proprietary code, which means it won't validate.

So what's the best way to add this attribute in Dreamweaver? I'm glad you asked. I suggest you add the attribute to the tags you need it for in the Tag Library Editor. Then you'll have the attribute available in the Attributes tab in Show List view. You'll also have the attribute available as a code hint should you choose to hand-code it. If you're unfamiliar with the Tag Library Editor, see the "Create Your Own Code Hints" tip in Chapter 9.

   ## ARCHIVES, EMULATORS, AND VIEWERS, OH MY!

You too can become a browser-
testing fanatic. For all your
development testing needs, a
collection of varying browser
versions have been archived at
Evolt: http://www.dwkillertips
.com/go/24. Do you ever wonder what your webpage looks
like on a version 2.0 browser?
Don't bother installing an old
browser just to satisfy your
curiosity. Instead, head on over
to a site that specializes in
browser emulation such as Deja
Vu: http://www.dwkillertips

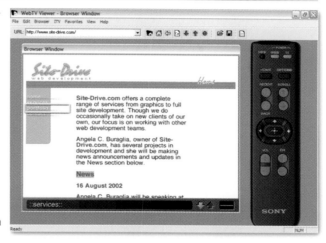

.com/go/27. If a client is concerned with Web TV, you needn't worry about buying a Web TV
box just for his site developement. There's the Web TV Viewer available for testing your websites: http://www.dwkillertips/com/go/28.

   ## LEARNING TO ACCESSORIZE

You don't need to be a fashion diva to
accessorize your browser with trendy, hip,
cool features. Adding accessories to your
browser will make surfing easier and testing
websites much quicker and cleaner. You'll be
able to make a selection, right-click, and
select View Partial Source, which will show
you the source code of only your selection.
No more scrolling through endless lines of
code to find the single line you need. That's
just one of many features you can add to
your browser. No matter how I describe the
features, you can't get a clear picture of their
usefulness without trying them first. You can

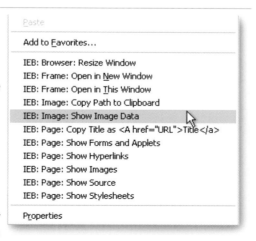

find the accessories at two locations that I know of, depending on the flavor of Internet
Explorer you're running. Internet Explorer 5.x: http://www.dwkillertips.com/go/29. Internet
Explorer 5.5 and up: http://www.dwkillertips/go/30.

    ONLY TEMPORARY

When you are viewing a page in the browser using Dreamweaver's Preview in Browser feature, either the real page or a temporary file is displayed, depending on the setting in your
Preferences. Some folks just don't like temporary files, even though they're great for restor-
ing to a previous version if you screw up or crash. Since Dreamweaver MX, you're no longer
confined to using temporary files for browser previews. Deselect the check box labeled
Preview Using Temporary File in the Preview in Browser category of Edit > Preferences
(Dreamweaver > Preferences). The setting also affects Server Debugging used with
ColdFusion, which lets you use Dreamweaver's interface as a browser.

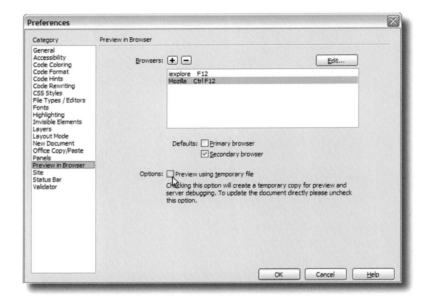

USER-DEFINED STYLES

As modern browsers make it easier for people to use their own custom style sheet on any given site, it is becoming increasingly important that you design your pages to good (X)HTML standards. In Mozilla, there is even a View > Use Style submenu, and Safari has an option in the Advanced category of its Preferences to specify your own style sheet. In Internet Explorer, select Tools > Internet Options, and then click the Accessibility button. In the dialog that appears, you can browse to a specific CSS file on your hard drive or point to an absolute URL. You can test local changes you've made to a site's CSS by setting the file as your user-defined CSS file. Make and save the modifications to your local file, and you can view the site online without disrupting the look until you're ready to replace the current file. Have fun with this one; you'll find it is a great way to learn all about CSS.

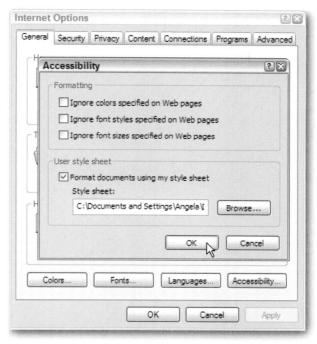

Design-O-Mite!

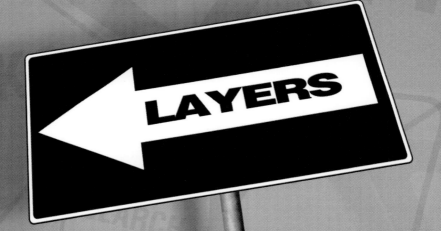

LAYERS

Dreamweaver users know "layers" as `<div>` *tags that use an absolute position defined within inline styles. Whether you call them layers or by any other*

Design-O-Mite!:
Explosive Layout Methods

name, it doesn't matter to me. (Hey, whatever makes you happy. I mean, you can call them shnicklegroobers for all I care, really.) But sooner or later you're going to need layers for a project and you're going to want to know all the coolest tips for using them in Dreamweaver. You may even get so inspired that you'll try to design your very first site without tables—unless you need to display tabular data, of course.

Frames have caused many developers I know to lose a few hairs and gain a few gray ones. Don't let this happen to you. Learn from our experiences and see how easy developing a frame-based site can be. Even if you don't like frames, you'll at the very least find some great entertainment value in these tips.

Now that you know what is in this chapter, why are you still reading this introduction? Go on, turn the page and indulge yourself in the wealth of knowledge that awaits you. <sigh> You're still reading this…</sigh> Fine, I'll just end this introduction right now so that you can stop wasting time and get on with the chapter.

   CHANGING LAYER STACKING ORDER

A layer's stacking order is controlled by the z-index. The higher the z-index, the closer to the front the layer appears in the browser. When you are working with multiple layers and need to change the z-index property, you will find that using the Property inspector can be a bit monotonous and tedious. The Layers panel (choose Window > Layers, or press F2) makes changing the z-index much easier. Click and drag the layer name within the Layers panel to where you want the layer to appear, and, automatically, each layer's z-index property will be adjusted to the new order. If you want to change a single layer's z-index without affecting the other layers, click the number in the Z column and type the new z-index value. When you're done, either press Enter (Return) or click elsewhere in the workspace.

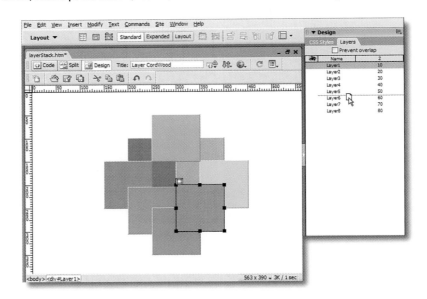

   DRAWING MULTIPLE CONSECUTIVE LAYERS

Often when I am working with layers, I need to draw several at once. I used to click the Draw Layer button in the Common category of the Insert bar (way back when it was called the Objects panel), draw my layer, and then repeat. Click button, draw layer. Click button, draw layer. That got old real quick. I soon discovered that there is indeed a better way to do this. All you need to do is hold the Ctrl (Command) key while clicking and dragging out your layer, and when you are finished, you'll still have the crosshairs that indicate you can draw another one.

LAYERS LIKE YOU LIKE 'EM

Adding a layer is simple when you use the Insert > Layout Objects > Layer command or the Draw Layer object found in the Layout category of the Insert bar. After inserting a layer, chances are that you'll need to make changes to its styles using the Property inspector. What you may not know is that you can save yourself the time and trouble of doing the same changes with each layer by setting your Layer preferences. Select Edit > Preferences (Dreamweaver > Preferences) or press Ctrl+U (Command+U), and then choose the Layers category from the list on the left. There you'll find various settings that will be used when you insert a layer. The Width and Height fields affect only layers that you insert with the Insert > Layout Objects > Layer command. Change this preference as often as you like to help speed up your layer production.

TAKING PREVENTATIVE MEASURES

If you decide to use the Layer Property inspector to change the values of Width, Height, Left, or Top, be sure to include a pixel or percentage measurement with the integer. Dreamweaver doesn't require that you enter a

unit of measurement, but modern browsers that support DTD will not respond well if the measurement is missing. So if you're experiencing placement issues in a browser, one of the first things to check is that the measurement for the property was included.

  MOVIN' AND GROOVIN' AND LAYIN' TO THE BEAT NOW

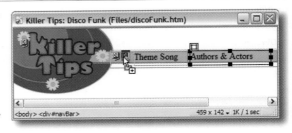

We were movin' and groovin' and jam-
ming to the beat, just when it hit me
and I heard somebody shout, "Drag
that layer by its shield now. Drag that
layer where you want!" Don't you sing
while you work? Assuming that you
know the tune "Play That Funky Music,
White Boy" by Wild Cherry, you'll
never be able to drag a layer by its
shield again without thinking of this tip. When you have a layer selected, its corresponding
anchor point (that little yellow shield-looking thingy) also is highlighted. If you click and drag
the layer by its anchor point, the corresponding code is moved right along with it, effectively
changing the order of your code and shields. If you don't see what I'm talking about, make
sure that View > Visual Aids > Invisible Elements is enabled. If you've previously disabled
them, turn on Invisible Elements for Anchor Points for Layers in Preferences.

   NO SPECIAL MAGIC REQUIRED

You needn't be a DHTML wizard to
show and hide layers. Dreamweaver
makes it easy with the Show-Hide
Layers behavior. Draw a layer where
you want it to appear. While you
have the link that will trigger the
event—be it text or an image—click
the Add (+) button on the Behaviors panel and then select the Show-Hide Layers behavior
from the drop-down list. Each layer is listed by its ID in the Named Layers field. Select each
layer that you want to reveal or conceal and then click the Show or Hide button. The Default
button resets the layer so that its current state is unchanged by this event. Just think of all
the cool menus you can create using this behavior. If you find yourself managing more than
four layers with this behavior often, be sure to check out "Show More Layers" in Chapter 10.

PUT THOSE LAYERS IN THEIR PLACE

Check out a Dreamweaver-generated page designed with Layers in Netscape 4.x and then change the size of your browser window. Notice that the page reloads? Dreamweaver adds what is known as the Netscape Resize Fix script to the page whenever a layer is inserted or drawn. Without this script, layers would not be in their proper place when users resize their browsers, which can get pretty messy. Dreamweaver doesn't add the script if you've inserted a `<div>` that has its positioning declared in the `<head>` of your page or in an external CSS file; it only knows to add it if the CSS is inline. You'll find the Add/Remove Netscape Resize Fix in the Commands menu—which will ask whether you want to add the script if it is not already on the page; otherwise, it asks whether you want to remove the script. If you decide to put the script in an external JavaScript file, you may want to visit the Layers category of Edit > Preferences (Dreamweaver > Preferences) to disable the automatic insertion of the code each time a layer is inserted by Dreamweaver.

SUPER SIZING LAYERS

When I lack the hand-eye coordination it takes to perfectly size layers by their resize handles, I switch to using keyboard shortcuts. With a layer already selected, I use Ctrl+Any arrow key (Option+Any arrow key) to size the layer pixel by pixel. For extra fun, try using Ctrl+Shift+Any arrow key (Option+Shift+Any arrow key) to change the layer's size by 10-pixel increments. If you've enabled View > Grid > Snap to Grid, the shortcuts mentioned here work together with

that feature, providing similar results and perhaps even speeding things up for you more. Dreamweaver is even smart enough to update your style sheet if you've defined the width and height externally.

   NO TRESPASSING

When you don't want to allow other layers to overlap existing layers, you don't have to do any math to calculate positioning. Even if it is simple addition and subtraction, who wants to do math? There is a special command that you can enable and disable as needed that will prevent layers inserted with the Draw Layer object from overlapping for you. You'll see a black circle with a line through it if you try to add a layer where a layer already exists. If you drag an existing layer, Dreamweaver won't let you trespass on other layer positions either. The Prevent Layer Overlaps command is rather hidden in the Modify > Arrange submenu. A more convenient location is at the top of the Layers panel, where you'll find a Prevent Overlaps check box.

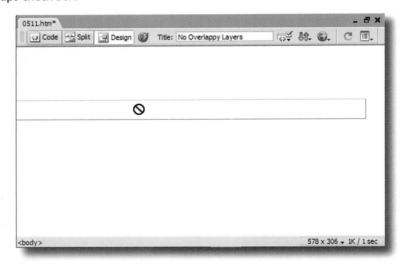

NESTING URGES

Feeling the urge to nest some layers? So long as you don't allow trespassers (see the earlier tip, "No Trespassing"), you can use a few techniques to make the process painless. Hold down the Alt (Option) key while clicking and dragging over another layer for an easy approach to nesting layers. If you will be doing a lot of nesting, there is a Preference setting you should know about. Select Edit > Preferences (Dreamweaver > Preferences) or press Ctrl+U (Command+U), and then choose the Layers category listed on the left. Notice the check box labeled "Nest when created within a layer"? If that check box is marked, whenever you start to draw a layer with the Draw Layer object while your cursor is over another layer—even without holding the Alt (Option) key—the new layer will end up nested inside the existing layer. Another approach to nesting layers is to click inside a layer, and then choose Insert > Layout Objects > Layer. There you have it: Three ways to nest a layer using Dreamweaver. Not enough, you say? You want another method? Okay, how about Ctrl+Click-n-Drag (Command+Click-n-Drag) the name of an existing layer in the panel and release the mouse key when the layer is over what will become the parent layer. You'll know you've got it right when you see the Layers panel listing layers in a tree-menu type of format.

THE OBVIOUS ESCAPES US SOMETIMES

If you're like me, sometimes the obvious escapes you—pun very much intended, as you'll soon see. After you click that Draw Layer icon, you're stuck with the crosshairs until you draw a layer. However, if you press the Esc key, you'll be freed from that cursor and won't have to draw a layer after all. A single click in the document without dragging also frees you of the cursor. I'd rather use the Esc key than go through the process of adding something unwanted only to undo it. In fact, using the Esc key has the same cancellation effect for most situations in Dreamweaver in which you might change your mind.

     CHANGE LAYER CONTENTS

There is no need to make the user wait for an entire new page to load when all you want to change is just a single layer's contents. Don't let the name fool you; the Set Text of Layer behavior does more than change text in a layer. You need at least one layer on the page before you

can click the Behaviors panel's Add (+) button and select Set Text > Set Text of Layer. In the dialog that appears, notice that it says New HTML. Try using any HTML you want, and as long as the browser understands it, that code will be represented in the layer after you click OK. Be sure that the event listed in the Behaviors panel is set the way you want it, and then go ahead and preview the page.

"Why not use Show/Hide Layers and use as many layers as needed?" One benefit is that the layer will always have the same ID and other attributes. This means that the look of the layer can remain consistent without repeating the same code.

     INSERT DIV TAG

Creating table-less designs in Dreamweaver just got a whole lot easier with the Insert DIV Tag object. If you're not familiar with ID selectors, you'll want to check out "Can I See Some Identification, Please?" tip in Chapter 2 before you continue with this tip. The Insert DIV Tag object lets you place `<div>` tags at the insertion point, relative to other tags that have an ID; if no other tags have an ID, you can place the `<div>` tag relative to the `<body>`. Be sure that you've linked your CSS file (or have some embedded) so that the Class and ID list can be populated for you. If the class or ID you'd like to set aren't listed, just type in your own. You can even use this object to insert just the `<div>` tag by leaving the Class and ID fields blank.

   FRAMESETS-A-PALOOZA

If you've used any of the Frames objects in previous versions, you know that Dreamweaver incorporates the current page into the created frameset. But what if you are starting from scratch, know you want a particular style of frameset, but you don't have a page to start with? Before Dreamweaver MX, you had to open a blank page and apply a Frames object; now you can skip that intermediate step and open a new frameset page and be ready to go. Dreamweaver's New Document dialog includes a Framesets category with all the same formats available as Frames objects—as well as two more: Split Horizontal and Split Vertical. Just choose one and Dreamweaver creates all the pages you need, leaving your current page alone.

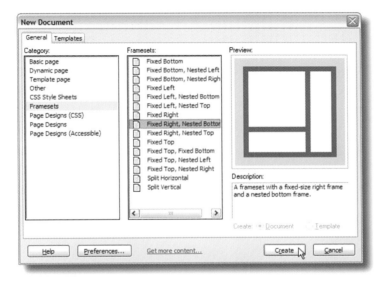

   ## SPLITS ARE ALL RELATIVE

Almost all the standard framesets created by the Frames objects or the New Document dialog involve one or more frames with a set pixel width or height. Put in a Fixed Left frameset,
for example, and the left frame has a width of 80 pixels. (For whatever reason, 80 seems to
be one of the Dreamweaver engineers' favorite numbers—all the frames with set values are
set to 80 pixels.) The two exceptions to the set pattern are the Split Horizontal and Split
Vertical framesets. Apply either of these frame objects and your page is—well, split—into
two sections, both using the relative measurement. This brings me to the "gotcha!"—resize
either of these split framesets and, instead of one or both frames switching to a fixed pixel
width, they both remain listed with relative values. Depending on the size of your frames,
this could mean that some of your content might not be seen on smaller browser windows.
(By the way, you can get into the same spot of trouble by choosing any of the Split Frame
options under Modify > Frameset.) The solution here is to select the frameset and, from the
Frames Property inspector, change one of the frames from Relative to Pixels units.

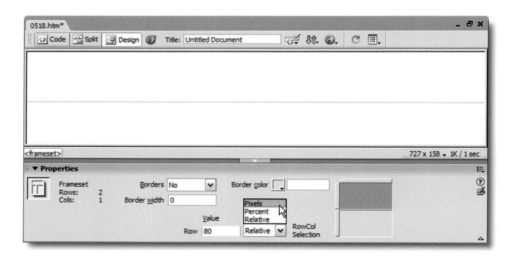

QUICK DRAW FRAMESETS

The Frames objects are pretty swift—in fact, they're so nifty, many folks don't realize that you can drag out a frameset manually. To create a frameset by dragging, choose View > Visual Aids > Frame Borders (or select the same menu option from the View Options button on the Document toolbar). Then, hold Alt (Option) while you drag out one of the borders. You even can instantly create a frameset with four frames by dragging in the frame border corner—try that, Frames objects!

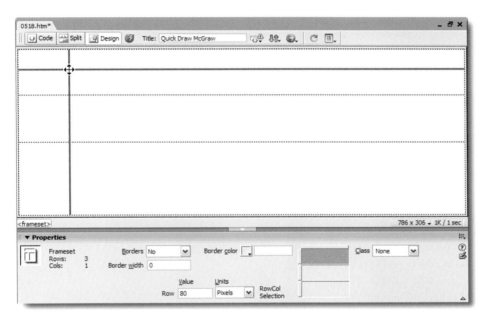

   WHY SO BLUE?

Ever wonder why the icons representing the Frame objects found in the Layout category of the Insert bar look the way they do? Every icon has one area shown in a light blue color. Sure, it's stylish—but it's also purposeful. The blue area represents where the current page is placed when a Frame object is applied. So the first icon, called Left Frame, places your existing content on the right and the second icon, called Right Frame, puts the current page on the left. I find the object names somewhat misleading (yeah, like BMW's are somewhat expensive), so I just go by the icon to pick the style I want.

   GETTING IN TOUCH WITH YOUR INNER FRAMESET

Nested framesets are often the best choice for a complex layout—but they can be difficult to modify. The key to making changes to a nested frameset is choosing the right one. You'll find the key at the bottom of the window in the area called the tag selector. Click any frameset border to identify which frameset you're using. If you see only one `<frameset>` tag in the tag selector, you've selected the outermost frameset. Select another

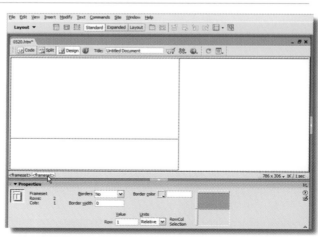

border, and when you see two `<frameset>` tags, choose the rightmost one to select the inner frameset. With an extremely complex layout—say, three or more nested framesets—you may have to select a few different borders to identify the desired frameset.

     PLAYING THE FRAME NAME GAME

Everyone who has worked with frames has had this experience. You start work on your frameset and get far enough along that you're ready to preview the page, so you press F12, Preview in Browser. Dreamweaver requires that all elements—each of the pages and the frameset(s)—be saved before previewing, so the Save File dialog box pops up. But how do you name a file if you don't know which file you're naming? The preset names (`Untitled-7.htm`, `Untitled-8.htm`, and so on) are not much help. Luckily, Dreamweaver gives you a couple of clues, if you know where to look. Framesets are always saved first, and a special generic name is used: `UntitledFrameset-X`, where `X` represents an incrementing number. The biggest clue, however, is visual: Dreamweaver identifies what frame it is asking you to save by placing a dotted, black border around the frame in the Document window. If it is a frameset (nested or otherwise), more than one frame is enclosed.

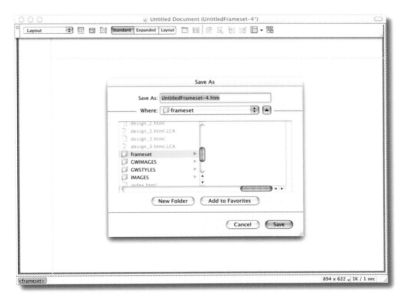

  A FRAMESET BY ANY OTHER NAMESET

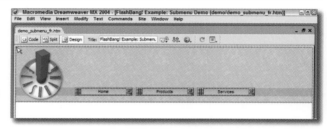

How many times have you been surfing the web and come across a frame-based page where the browser window displays "Untitled Documents"? How many times has that been one of your sites? Incorrectly titling a frameset is a fairly common mistake—many times, designers give one of the frames the desired title instead of the frameset, which is where is needs to be. Before entering the title in Dreamweaver's Document toolbar, make sure that you've selected the frameset border. When you go back to entering content in one of the frames, the title will disappear—but that's to be expected. Select the frameset border again and the title will reappear in Dreamweaver and be there when the pages are uploaded to the web.

   KEEPING FRAMES IN THEIR PLACE

Because framesets are comprised of separate pages, it's entirely possible for a user to browse directly to a page—from a search engine, for example—and have no idea it's supposed to be part of a frameset. One way to handle this problem is to put this code in the `<head>` of every file in the frameset:

```
<script language="JavaScript">
if (top == self) self.location.href = "FramesetFileName";
</script>
```

In this code, `FramesetFileName` is the name of the frameset the file is part of. This code looks to see whether the page is within a frameset and if not, puts it in its intended place. Notice that this code is triggered only if the page is not in a frameset; it doesn't determine whether or not it is in the correct frameset.

 ## HELP, I'VE BEEN FRAMED, AGAIN!

Framed against your will? How do you keep your pages from being frame-napped and placed in someone else's frameset? Here's the JavaScript to place in pages you want to keep frameless:

```
<script language="JavaScript">
if (self.parent.frames.length!=0){
self.parent.location.replace(document.location.href)
}
</script>
```

If you want to keep your hand-coding to a minimum, another solution is to add the Thierry Koblentz Break Out Of Frames extension (available from the Dreamweaver Exchange) to your page. Not adverse to a minimum of handiwork? Turn the preceding code into a snippet and apply at your leisure.

 ## TARGETING MULTIPLE FRAMES

The vast majority of the time, a hyperlink in a frameset is intended to load a page in a single frame. Sometimes, however, a single hyperlink is needed to update multiple frames. There are two ways to approach this problem—although neither are worry free. The first method is to hyperlink to another frameset that corresponds to the targeted pages; this works well when the pages that are changing are associated. The only real negative is that it adds another layer of complexity to managing the site. The other method is to use a standard hyperlink in addition to a Dreamweaver Go To URL behavior—the hyperlink opens one page in a targeted frame, and the behavior opens another page in a different frame. The downside to the second approach is that it takes two clicks of the browser's Back button for the user to return to the previous location.

     OODLES OF UNDO-ODLES

If you know anything about frames, you know that each frameset is made up of multiple files—but here's something you may not realize: Each of the frames has an independent undo memory or stack. This means that you can make a change in one of your frames, switch to another, select Undo from the Edit menu, or press Ctrl+Z (Command+Z), and the change in the other frame will not be undone. You must select the frame containing the change you want reversed. A graphical way to see this is to open the History panel (Window > History) and then click into each and every one of your frames—the History panel displays different steps for every one. Even the frameset itself, an independent HTML file, has its own undo stack.

Bonus tip: To undo the application of a frameset, after choosing one of the Frame objects, select Undo twice. The first Undo displays the page split vertically into two frames, and the second brings it back to a framesetless state, although the Dreamweaver-drawn frame borders are still visible around the document. You can turn those off by choosing View > Visual Aids > Frame Borders. Hey, that was a bonus, bonus tip!

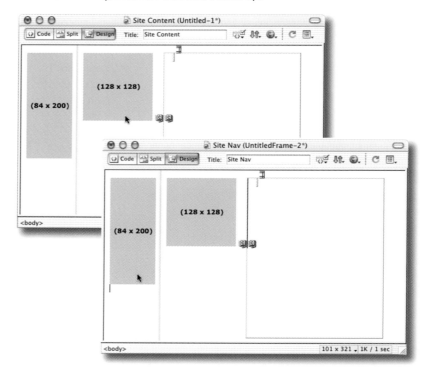

CREATING ACCESSIBLE FRAMES

The Section 508 accessibility guidelines require that frames be titled with under-standable names that assist navigation. The key word here is *titled*. It is not enough for your frames to have appropriate names, such as `navigation` or `content`; addi-tionally, each `<frame>` also must have a `title` attribute with similar values (the name and `title` attributes don't have to be the same, although that's often the easiest course). The `title` attribute can, of course, be added by hand or by selecting the `<frame>` tag in Code view and entering the `title` value in the Tag inspector. The other technique for making sure your frameset is compliant with Section 508 is to enable the Frames option in the Accessibility category of Preferences. Once enabled, the Frame Tag Accessibility Attributes dialog box appears whenever a frameset is created. To title the frames, choose the frame name from the drop-down list and enter the desired title in the bottom field; be sure to cycle through all the frame names. The Frame Tag Accessibility Attributes dialog box (say that five times fast!) does not appear, however, if you create the frameset by dragging out a frame border.

Frame Tag Accessibility Attributes

For each frame, specify a title.

Frame: mainFrame

Title: Main Biz

OK
Cancel
Help

   DÉJÀ VU FRAMES

Looking to play a trick on fellow web designers? Throw a little recursion their way. To make a recursive frame, first set a link on a frameset to the frameset itself. Next, set the target attribute of that link to `_self`. When selected, the page with the recursive link will be replaced by the entire frameset—which is already within the frameset. Select the link again and you've got a frameset within a frameset within a frameset. You can recursively display a frameset with about three or four iterations before they "blow up real good," as the boys on SCTV used to say. Of course, if you want to avoid recursive framesets, set that target to `_top`—but then you'd just be a spoilsport.

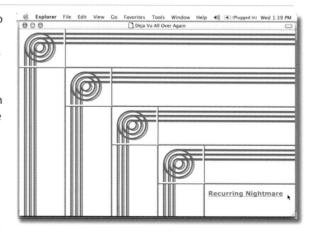

   THE GUIDING LIGHT

Guides are a layout feature I've always wanted in Dreamweaver; I find them incredibly helpful in other programs such as Fireworks. A guide is a vertical or horizontal line that enables
you to line up various elements in your design. Because Dreamweaver doesn't offer them, I
found a way to make my own using Dreamweaver `<div>` tags and the magic of CSS.

Driving the heart of our Dreamweaver guides are two CSS classes, which I've called
`.horzGuide` and `.vertGuide`. I've colored both guides a bright green and given them a
high z-index of 100 to stand out—and on top—of the rest of the page. The key to the horizontal guide style is to set the border-top property to 1 pixel and the width to 100%, like
this:

```
.horzGuide {
    border-top: 1px solid #00FF00;
    position:absolute;
    left:100px;
    top:0px;
    width:100%;
    z-index:100;
}
```

I've also started the guide out so that it is flush to the left side of the screen, and a standard
100 pixels in.

Vertical guides are similar, with two key properties altered. To go vertical, we'll set border-
left (or border-right, depending on your political leanings) instead of the horizontal guide's
border-top and making the height 100% rather than width:

```
.vertGuide {
    border-left: 1px solid #00FF00;
    position:absolute;
    left:0px;
    top:100px;
    height:100%;
    z-index:100;
}
```

Now for the fun part—not that setting up CSS classes isn't a riot. Create a `<div>` tag by
choosing Insert `<div>` Tag from the Insert bar's Layout category. When the `<div>` tag dialog pops up, choose either `horzGuide` or `vertGuide` from the Class list and there you go!

One additional helpful step is to deselect View > Visual Aids > Layer Borders so that when
the guides are not selected, all you see are the lines. Hey, how 'bout some props for the
guide master?

After the `<div>` is on the page, you can move it in a bunch of ways. Because it's a position-able `<div>` (a.k.a. a layer in Dreamweaver-speak), you can drag it wherever you like. Selected `<div>` tags can be moved using the arrow keys, one pixel at a time or, with the Shift key pressed, 10 pixels at a time. For an exact pixel placement, change the Left or Top fields on the Property inspector.

Because the CSS rules are set up as classes rather than IDs, you can create as many vertical and horizontal guides as you need. Store your CSS in an external style sheet and use the Design Time Style Sheet feature to turn it on whenever you need a little guidance.

Assembly Line Acceleration

Template Library

Are you the kind of web designer who lovingly crafts each bit of code that goes into the page? Someone who, if you could, would sculpt the angle brackets

Assembly-Line Acceleration:
Rapid Template, Library, and Page Production

that surround each HTML tag? If that description fits you like a wet t-shirt, then skip right over this chapter. This chapter is for working folks, designers who need to get the job done—get it done right, of course—the most efficient way possible. Because the web designer's job is an on-going one, implementing the design and updating the site must be as easy and thorough as possible. If that sounds like Dreamweaver templates and library items to you, you're in the right place. You want to know how much of a geek I am? When Macromedia added repeating and optional regions as well as editable attributes, I partied for three days—and believe me, Dreamweaver geeks know how to party.

Throughout this chapter, you'll find tips detailing how best to use these advanced features and more (we threw in some general production tips for good measure). By this chapter's end, I expect to see you whipping out templates with one hand, inserting library items with the other, while dancing an Irish jig. Or maybe a Texas two-step…anything but that Macarena dance; I'm flexible…to a point.

   KEEPING IT STYLISH

Part of the reason templates have proved so popular is that they enable the designer to specify a consistent look and feel while allowing the content to vary. If you're not careful how you define your editable regions in templates, however, you could lose the control over style. When selecting the content for an editable region, be careful not to include any formatting elements that could be altered. If you want to make sure that your heading remains a

`<h3>` style, for example, select only the text within the tag, not the tag itself. If you include the `<h3>...</h3>` tag pair, it could easily be changed to another heading style in the document derived from the template. I frequently stay in the split-view mode to see both code and the design elements and ensure that I have selected only what I want to remain editable. This tip is doubly important in the new-world order of CSS where a heading could be specified like this: `<h3 id="mainheading">`. Also when using CSS, 99.9% of the time the style sheet declarations (whether you are working with external or internal styles) should remain in the locked part of the template.

   EDIBLE PEARS VERSUS EDITABLE PAIRS

When you're marking an area of your document as an editable region, you need to make sure that you're working with complete tag pairs. You either need to select content within a tag pair, or select the tag pair itself. If you don't, Dreamweaver expands the selection until its overlapping tags are enclosed before applying the editable region—and there's no warning that your selection isn't proper. For example, let's say you want to make a column in a table editable. You'd think you would be able to choose the column and then select Editable Region from the Insert bar Templates category, right? Wrong. The column designation has no equivalent in HTML tags, and so Dreamweaver marks as editable all the rows containing cells within the selected column. The right, albeit tedious, way to make a column editable is to separately mark each cell (`<td>...</td>`) in the column as an editable region.

SECRET TEMPLATES

I've known a devious developer or three who use Dreamweaver's template feature, but their clients would never know it. They're the only person working on the site, so changes are never made to the files that are on the server by anyone else. Why do they hide it? They didn't charge the client for a template, and in the event someone else becomes the webmaster they won't gain the benefits. Perhaps there are other reasons, but I'll just let you think of them while I show you how to get rid of all that template markup.

What you do is keep a local site with the template markup intact and make template changes as needed. Next use Modify > Templates > Export without Markup to strip out template markup from the entire site. Upload changes from the markup-free site.

   DA LINK'S DA TING

What's the number-one problem folks have with templates? Links. Web designers used to coding links by hand are frequently tripped up when working with templates. Here's why: When a document is derived from the template, Dreamweaver automatically adjusts the links so that they point to the proper file. But for Dreamweaver to handle this operation correctly, the links must point to the right file from the template itself (which is stored in the Templates folder, in the site root). A common mistake is to try to create a link to a file as though the template were the derived document. Here's an example. Let's say famed designer Joe Schmoe is working with a Dreamweaver template and creates a link to a widgets.html page in the Products folder. Joe thinks, "I know the pages I'm going to create from this template will all be located in the root folder, and the Products folder is also in the root, so I'll just write in the link like this, Products/widgets.html." I'm afraid Mr. Schmoe has made a *faux pas*. The correct link in the template would be ../Products/widgets.html—which Dreamweaver would convert to Products/widgets.html in a document derived from the template. The best way to ensure that you are assigning the correct links in a template is to always use the Browse for File or Point to File options found on the Property inspector next to the Link field. If you're linking to a file that doesn't exist yet, use Browse for File to link to another file in the same folder and change the file's name by hand.

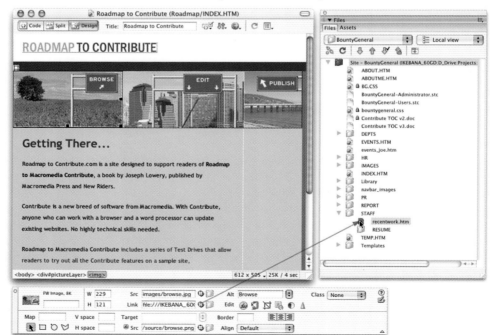

   I NEVER META TEMPLATE PARAMETER I DIDN'T LIKE

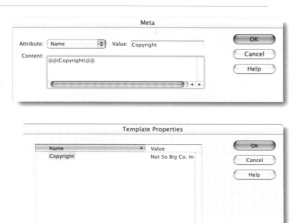

Pragmatically speaking, descriptive `<meta>` tags are key to authoring refreshing, nonrobotic web pages, whether basic standalone or linked to external sites. (Did you catch all the references to the different `<meta>` tag types in that opening sentence? I once did the same thing naming the varieties of pickles with my girlfriend; you try working "tiny gherkins" into a sentence and see how far you get.) If you're designing a template and you want to make it possible for the user to add values to particular `<meta>` tags, you can expose them through template parameters. The major benefit to using template parameters with `<meta>` tags is that it ensures that the `<meta>` tag is not accidentally deleted—an all-too-real possibility if you enclose the tags in an editable region. Another advantage is that Contribute users can add to `<meta>` tags more than just keywords and description.

Adding template parameters to a `<meta>` tag is a two-step process. First you need to insert a template parameter statement into the `<head>` of the document. Let's say we want to add the ability to insert a copyright notice. In this case, the template parameter would look like this:

```
<!-- TemplateParam name="Copyright" type="text" content="BigCo, Inc." -->
```

The name parameter is arbitrary, but should be reflective of the type of `<meta>` tag used. The initial content can either be a placeholder you would actually use or a more generic "Enter Company Name Here." The problem with the latter approach is that if the user doesn't change the template parameter, that's what is going on the page.

The second part is the `<meta>` tag itself, substituting the template parameter variable for the content value:

```
<meta name="copyright" content="@@(Copyright)@@">
```

After these changes have been saved and the child pages created, the `<meta>` tag is accessible both in Dreamweaver (from Modify > Template Properties) and Contribute (Format > Template Properties). Don't you just relish tips like these? They're my bread and butter.

CHAPTER 6 • Rapid Template, Library, and Page Production **123**

NESTED TEMPLATE LOCKING

One of my favorite moments is when you first create a new editable region in a nested template. Not only is your new editable region outlined in good old reliable blue, but the base template's editable region also turns orange (tell any non-geek I said that, and I'll deny it to my dying day). That works just swell for locking part of an editable region and keeping the other part open. However, what if you want to lock the entire region for a particular nested template while keeping it available for others? Not a problem—all you need is an unassociated template variable. Normally, a template variable looks like this: `@@(bgcolor)@@`. If you leave out the variable name and insert the code anywhere in the editable region, however, the entire editable region is locked for all children of the nested template. In other words, you would change code like this:

```
<!-- InstanceBeginEditable name="guidelines" -->
<h2>New Administrative Guidelines Now in Effect </h2>
<!-- InstanceEndEditable -->
```

And turn it into code like this:

```
<!-- InstanceBeginEditable name="guidelines" -->
<h2>@@(" ")@@New Administrative Guidelines Now in Effect </h2>
<!-- InstanceEndEditable -->
```

The unassociated template variable locks down the editable region tighter than a drum for pages derived from this nested template, without slamming the door shut for them all.

   QUICK EDITABLE REGIONS

When building a template from scratch, you can quickly add editable regions without having to select any existing content—a handy trick 'cause sometimes the content doesn't exist yet. Just position the cursor where you'd like the editable region to appear and choose Insert > Template

Objects > Editable Region. If you're feeling dexterous, choose Ctrl+Alt+V (Command+Option+V). Want to point and click? Select the Editable Region object from the Templates menu in the Common category of the Insert bar. All these methods give you a chance to name the region and then put that name, as text, in the editable region. If I'm passing the template on to someone else, I try to replace the text—which also appears in the identifying tab—with something more meaningful, such as "Bio info on author goes here." One other note on working with Dreamweaver-inserted editable regions: If you decide to remove the region, the included text stays behind and becomes part of your locked template, which means that you'll have to delete that text manually.

   FOL NOT SOL

Ever hear the acronym FOL? It stands for "fact of life," and that's what you encounter if you try to draw a layer in an editable region. This particular FOL takes the form of an alert that making this change would mean changing locked code, and Dreamweaver ain't gonna do it. Okay, okay, no hard feelings—so how do you insert a layer in an editable region? Actually there are two roads around this particular FOL. One way is to place your cursor in the editable region and use the menu command Insert > Layout Objects > Layers; then you can modify the layer via the sizing handles or using the Property inspector. The other route is to use the Insert Div Tag object from the Layout category of the Insert bar and modify to your heart's content. And them's the facts, Jack.

   CHANGING YOUR MIND ABOUT TEMPLATE REGIONS

Let me fill you in on some tips to keep in mind when deleting template markup. First off, do you know how to convert an editable region back to a locked area? Place your cursor within the editable region and choose Modify > Templates > Remove Template Markup; this option also is available from the Templates section of the context menu. The same process is used to get rid of an optional or a repeating region. It's also handy to note when removing an optional region that the region's corresponding `TemplateParam` statement is not removed. You'll have to hunt down those little buggers and axe 'em yourself.

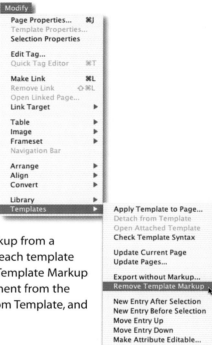

Finally, how do you get rid of all the template markup from a page? Although you could go through and select each template region individually, and then choose the Remove Template Markup command, a far faster method is to create a document from the template, choose Modify > Templates > Detach from Template, and then save the new document over your old.

   ## JUST THE HIGHLIGHTS, PLEASE

It's gotten a whole lot easier to find those `<div>` tags on the screen now that mouse-over highlighting has been put into play. Although there aren't too many situations where the bright red highlight won't stand out, you do have an option to change the color if necessary. Head on over to the Highlighting category in Edit > Preferences (Dreamweaver > Preferences) and select whatever color suits your fancy for the Mouse-Over option. Of course, if you're at a point where the mouse-over highlighting is more distraction than help, deselect the Show check box next to Mouse-Over. The same option controls mouse-over highlighting for tables as well as drawn layers and `<div>` tags.

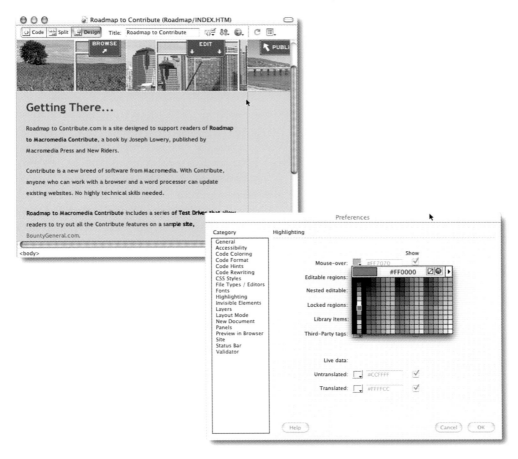

   EDITABLE ATTRIBUTES BLAST OFF

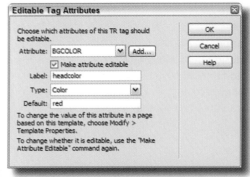

I've got a warm spot by the bed for editable attributes. With this feature (accessible by choosing Modify > Templates > Make Attribute Editable), you can unlock only the essential aspects of an object, such as a table row's background color, while keeping everything else (the alignment, the class, and so on) safe and secure. Editable attributes also enable you to unlock aspects of a tag while keeping the enclosed content nailed down. For all their power, there is a bit of a learning curve in figuring out how to best work with editable attributes. Here's a tip that will help you skip a couple of steps in the setup process. Whenever possible, make sure that your tag already includes the attribute you plan to make editable. Although the Editable Tag Attributes dialog enables you to add any attribute you want, if the attribute is already in the tag—whether or not it has a value—you can simply pick it from a drop-down list. Otherwise, you have to choose Add and fill in the attribute name.

   SHARING THE LIBRARY CARD

When working with library items, I often find that what works well in one site can also be used in another. Dreamweaver includes a rather zippy facility for just these occasions: Copy to Site. From the Library category of the Assets panel, first select the Options menu and choose Copy to Site. Then, from the submenu, select the site you want to copy the library item to. Be careful, however: Only the library item itself is copied. Any dependent files that the library item relies on, such as images or Flash movies, need to be transferred manually.

EDITABLE ATTRIBUTES, TWO FOR TWO

Here are a couple more pointers worth sharing that can help you work with editable attributes. Numerous attributes—such as width or height—require a numeric value, or what appears to be a numeric value. Because the attributes could actually be a percent or pixel designation, such as 75%, the value is really text. Therefore, when you are setting up your editable attributes in a template, specify the type as Text rather than Number. If you choose Number and try to enter a percentage or pixel value, Dreamweaver will bark at you when you save the template.

Ready for another tidbit? After you establish an editable attribute, you can apply it to as many tags as you like. This capability is quite handy when you want various elements on the page to share a characteristic. You could, for example, change the background image of a table cell on multiple tables. To apply the attribute in various tags, just copy and paste the attribute that includes the template variable.

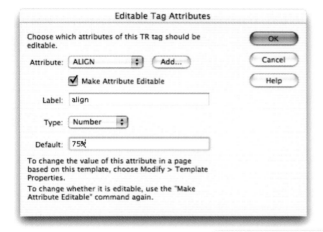

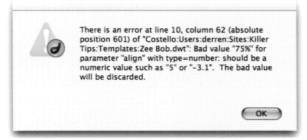

    THE DARK SIDE OF EDITABLE ATTRIBUTES

Okay, so I've waxed poetic about editable attributes for the last couple of tips. Does sliced bread still wear the crown as the coolest thing? Unfortunately, yes. You should also note that, in my view, editable attributes have a significant design flaw: After you make an attribute editable, it no longer is rendered when editing the template. Suppose, for example, that you make the background color of a table cell editable—you even choose a reasonable default color. When editing the template, the attribute will look like this: `bgcolor= "@@(tdcolor)@@"`. Dreamweaver doesn't properly interpret the variable name as the `bgcolor` value (unlike with template instances), so it acts as if it isn't there. This is particularly noticeable when your design actually includes the attribute. Unfortunately, there's really not a workaround for this problem. You can, however, kvetch about it by writing wish-dreamweaver@macromedia.com and gain a minor bit of satisfaction.

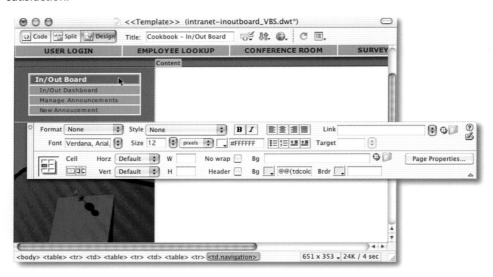

   ALTERNATING ROW COLORS, THE TEMPLATE PARAMETER WAY

Template expressions are another nifty addition to template power introduced in Dreamweaver MX. One extremely useful technique is establishing an alternating background color within a repeating region. After you've set up your repeating region in a template table, select the `<tr>` tag that repeats (you could also use a `<p>` tag) and enter Code view. Add this attribute to the tag:

```
bgcolor="@@((_index & 1) ?
'#FFFFFF' : '#FFFF99')@@"
```

This particular code alternates a white and light yellow background; you can, of course, substitute any other color values you want. But what if you want to alternate every two rows or—heavens to Betsy!— every three rows? Change the number value included in the parentheses with the `_index` keyword (1 in the original code) to 2 or—gasp!—4. (Caveat templator: Some higher values, such as 3 and 5, offer not such predictable results. Test thoroughly.)

   THE HOBGOBLIN OF BIG MINDS

Updating Dreamweaver 4 templates can be a nightmarish chore, but there's a tool to scare away the design-time boogie man: the Inconsistent Region Names dialog. You'll see this dialog displayed whenever you're applying a new template to a page already based on a template and the regions do not match exactly, down to their case. You'll also see it when you attempt to apply a template to a regular document. Through this interface, Dreamweaver gives you the chance to map the content in a document to any region in the template. If

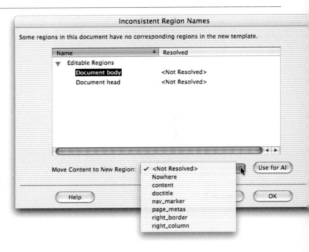

you realize you no longer need the content, you can discard it. You do, however, have to decide what to do with all the content; Dreamweaver refuses to budge until you make your choices clear.

   STYLIN' AT THE BIBLIOTHEQUE

I love working with library items and style sheets. There is something so gratifying about dropping what appears to be a plain-text element onto a page and, wham-o, you're looking good! Working the magic does take a fair degree of planning, however. Of primary importance is the need to make sure that the classes applied to your library item elements are included in your style sheet. Likewise, you want to be sure to define CSS rules for all the HTML tags used in the library items. One way to make sure that your bases are covered is to create the library item from a page where it is correctly styled. To keep you on your toes, Dreamweaver displays a warning that the style rules won't be included when you save the library item.

STAY TUNED FOR A SPECIAL UPDATE

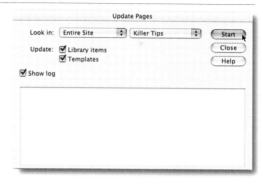

With both library items and templates, when you save the document, you are asked whether you want to update pages. Maybe you decided not to because maybe you realized you made a mistake or you have other updates planned. Perhaps you agreed to update files, but in the summary that follows an update, you notice a few files were not updated for whatever reason. In any case, if ever you need to redo an update, you can find the Update Current Page and Update Pages commands in the Modify menu under the Library and Templates submenus. You'll also find Update Current Page under the context menu and Options menu of the Templates and Library categories of the Assets panel, but instead of Update Pages you'll see Update Site—same thing, different name. Naturally these commands only work if a template or library item is already in use with a document. Which check box, Library or Templates, is checked depends on how you arrived at the dialog, but you can definitely choose both and make your updates lickety-split.

THE REGION NAME GAME

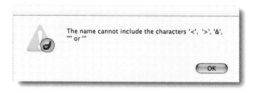

Does it matter what you name your template regions? Template region names are not as sensitive as other object names, such as those for layers or images, but there are limits. Certain special characters are not allowed: the ampersand (&), double quote ("), single quote a.k.a apostrophe ('), and the left and right angle brackets (< and >). You'll also want to avoid underscores (_) if you intend on doing any import or export of the template content to XML. Moreover, each region's name must be unique among other template regions in the same template. In other words, it's possible to have a layer and an editable region both named `content`. Is it a good idea? Probably not, but that's never stopped anyone before, so why should you be different?

   WHATEVER HAPPENED TO NEW FROM TEMPLATE...?

Back in the day of Dreamweaver 4, there was the File > New from Template command. Many have scoured the interface to find out how to make a new child page from a template. I told you back in Chapter 1 that there are context menus all over the place in Dreamweaver, some of which offer options available only in those very context menus. New from Template is one of those instances where you won't find another menu command of its kind (unless you've customized Dreamweaver or happen to own my Template-Lover's Suite of extensions available from the DWfaq.com store). Now that I've built you up with just a little anticipation, I'll tell you that New from Template is in the context menu of the Assets panel's Templates category. Another way to create a new page based on a template is to select File > New and select the Templates tab to choose a template from the list of sites and generate the new template-based page. Both of the methods I just described will do; the latter method I find faster than waiting for the Assets panel to initialize. However, I find that the customized menu offers the fastest way; so if you're brave enough, I'll show you how to do that in Chapter 10.

   ROLLOVER BEETHOVEN

Swap as many images as you like on a single event, but bear in mind that they should be relatively close to the triggering hyperlink. (Otherwise, the swap may happen offscreen and go unseen by the user.) Select the image or a hyperlink, click the Add (+) button on the Behaviors panel, and then select the Swap Image behavior from the list. For each listed image, you can browse to the image you'd like replaced when the `onMouseOver` event is triggered. Each image that is affected by the behavior will have an asterisk beside it in the list.

If the list is filled with unnamed `<img>` elements, it will be difficult to determine which images are which so that you can apply the behavior. If you name the images in the Property inspector by filling in the field to the left of the H (for height), you won't have that trouble.

   ## LAYOUT VIEW PEARLS OF WISDOM

Geared toward visual designers, Layout view enables you to draw tables in much the same way you would slice an image in an image editor such as Fireworks. Although Layout

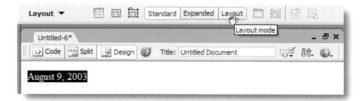

view made many improvements in Dreamweaver MX and a few since then, it isn't perfect. Never drag a table's border in Layout view or you run the risk of creating empty table cells, which in some browsers causes them to collapse and wreak havoc on your layout. The height attribute is invalid HTML and has a tendency to appear in table code created in Layout view.

Creating code blindly, without knowing what it does or whether it is correct, is an easy way to get in trouble. The best advice I can give for working in Layout view is to always work in Code and Design view so that you know what is going on with your code and only use it if you're well versed in HTML so that you can catch and correct the "gotchas" that are sometimes produced. Despite its flaws, Layout view can be great for quickly (in a matter of seconds) mocking up early design concepts that can be cleaned up later if needed.

   ## THE DOUBLE-CLICK FIX

When it comes time to make a change to a behavior—there always comes a time—you might be thinking that you'll have to remove the behavior and apply it again. That would be too much like work. Just locate the behavior in the Behaviors panel and double-click the event you need to modify. Well whaddaya know, the behavior's dialog appears with your current values set, enabling you to only modify the parameters you need to and be done.

  UNTITLED TIP

Unless you've made it a habit to title a document the moment you create it, chances are you've wound up with a stray untitled document in your site. Search Google.com for "untitled document" and you'll find well over 4 million results. I think this qualifies as an epidemic. Dreamweaver has a nifty feature that checks your entire site for untitled documents, and gives you a list of them so that you can take corrective measures. Choose Site > Reports, check Untitled Documents, and then click the Run button. All untitled documents in your site will appear in the Results panel. Double-click the file to open it, and then give the document a new title in the Document toolbar. You'll be doing your part to help prevent the spread of this plague of untitled documents on the web.

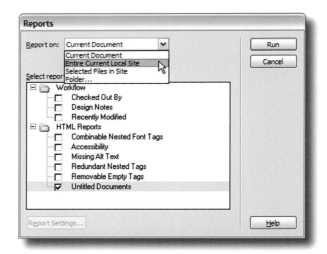

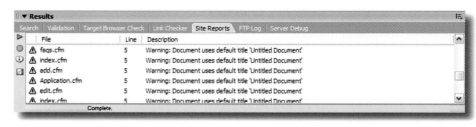

   ON THIS DATE

When you're unable to use server-side
scripting to determine when a file was last
modified, you can use Dreamweaver's Date
object (located in the Common category of the Insert
bar) to do this simply and effectively. This handy little
object can update the page with the current date—
and time, if you want it—of your computer's system
clock. When you add the object, you're given the
option to update the date each time you save the file.
This functionality is controlled by the comment tags
on each side of the date. If you're working in Code

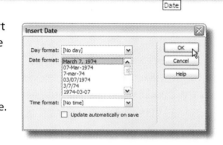

view, you can identify the comments by the `#BeginDate` and `#EndDate` before and after
the date, respectively. Any CSS formatting other than the date or additional text, such as
`Last Modified On:`, should not be added between these tags or you risk breaking the
functionality. If you're working in Design view and you select the date, Dreamweaver knows
to include the comment tags in the selection so that you can add formatting or drag it anywhere you like on the page. If you need to change the actual date, you can do so only manually in Code view. To change the format, first select the date in Design view, and then click
the Edit Date Format button on the Property inspector.

   XHTML, THE WAVE OF THE FUTURE

As you may know, HTML 4.01 is the latest version of HTML
and it is also the last version. HTML has been replaced with
XHTML, which isn't even one quarter as scary as it may
seem—especially with Dreamweaver's support for XHTML.
If you're starting from scratch, XHTML is pretty easy
because Dreamweaver detects the XHTML doctype and
makes an effort to write compliant code. You can give
HTML documents a quick transformation to XHTML by
using the File > Convert > XHTML command. After
Dreamweaver has made the changes, you may be alerted
that some images still need Alt text. You will have to add
the Alt text manually. Unless you're working in a file that
contains an XHTML doctype, Dreamweaver won't help you

write compliant code; so be extra careful to keep an eye on your code—"Do You Validate?"
in Chapter 9 will help you—especially when working in library item files or server-side
include files.

Miscellaneous Movers and Shakers

Increased Speed Ahead

Two web developer guys meet for lunch one Tuesday afternoon. "I need a vacation. Everything lately has been work, work, work…", complains the first guy.

Miscellaneous Movers and Shakers:

Dreamweaver's Cream of the Crop

The second guy says, "I know the feeling. I can't wait until next month. I'm going to Jamaica for a couple of weeks." The other developer responds, "Hey, that's not fair. You work on as many sites as I do. How can you afford to take the time off?" The second guy, looks down and notices Dreamweaver MX 2004 Killer Tips *sticking out of his briefcase and quickly pushes the briefcase under the table and—with a very big grin—he then replies, "I must work faster than you do." During lunch, the first guy gripes about typical web development woes while the second guy just smiles and nods.*

Hey, it could happen! This chapter is special—well they're all special, but this one is different—because this chapter is like a box of chocolates. That's right, you never know what you're going to get. You just might find that perfect tip that you didn't even know you were looking for that frees up so much of your time that you can afford to take that vacation you've been wanting. You never know; stranger things have happened! Send me an email if you need a good travel agent…

   YA WANT IT WITH OR WITHOUT?

By default, Dreamweaver now copies the formatting as well as the content when you copy a selection from a Microsoft Office document. Paste it in and the material is automatically converted into stripped-down HTML with such niceties as changing bold text to `<strong>` text. Just grab a paragraph or two from Word and Ctrl+V (Cmd+V) to paste it in—it's ready to go.

But what if you don't want the formatting? Simple enough: Choose Edit > Paste Text.

Although it doesn't have the convenience of a keyboard shortcut, you'll get your text straight-up and flying right. Line breaks come in as `<br>` tags, with two `<br>` tags for a single paragraph break in Word and `<p>` tags for double ones.

   FINDING YOUR ASSETS IN A DARK ROOM (WITHOUT A FLASHLIGHT)

I just love dragging images, Flash movies, and library items from the Assets panel and dropping onto the page. (By the way, did you know that the columns across the Assets panel can be used to sort the files? Click once to sort A–Z and again for Z–A.) Dreamweaver does a yeoman's job of keeping up with all the site elements, but it's not perfect by any means. Occasionally, you need to click the Refresh button to make Dreamweaver imported assets appear. Should you ever feel the urge to copy over assets in some other fashion—like with a file manager—you'll need to take it one step further. Instead of simply clicking the Refresh button, Ctrl+Click it (Command+Click) and you'll trigger the Recreate Site List command. True, it might take a moment, but it's the one way to be sure you're seeing all your site assets. Okay, okay, there's another way—choose Recreate Site List from the Assets panel Options menu.

WATCH OUT FOR KILLER OCTOTHORPES

How many times have you clicked a link to a pop-up window and found that when you closed the pop up, you're back at the top of the page again? Well, you've been attacked by an octothorpe, and I bet you didn't even know it! A what-o-thorpe, you ask? Octothorpe comes from the Greek word *octo*, which means eight. (If you've seen the movie *My Big Fat Greek Wedding*, you should know that all words come from a Greek word! Joe tells me that the *thorpe* part comes from James Oglethorpe, Georgia's founder. Should we believe him? The true origin is unknown according to the dictionary, so the world may never know….) Anyway, this is an octothorpe: #. You can call it the number sign, a hash, a pound sign, or any other words it may be known as, but I call 'em *octothorpes*. Octothorpes are great for some things, but not for creating what is known as a *null link*. So, as you use Dreamweaver's behaviors, keep an eye on the Link field of the Property inspector and make sure that you see `javascript:;` rather than an octothorpe. If you have a bunch of pages with null links you'd like to fix, you could use Dreamweaver's Find and Replace feature to search for this source code:

```
<a href="#"
```

And then replace it with this:

```
<a href="javascript:;"
```

This way you'll never subject your site's visitors to killer octothorpes again.

   KEEPING YOUR INCLUDES CONTRIBUTE-WORTHY

Any Server-Side Include (SSI) has potential to reduce your design workload by keeping consistent page elements such as navigation bars secure and easily modifiable. SSIs are pretty flexible, but you have to format them in a particular way to avoid problems when used in Contribute sites. Although it may be workable to split the `<head>` and/or `<body>` tags as far as your server is concerned, Contribute requires that all SSIs be self-contained. In other words, any SSI would have to be either within the `<head>` or the `<body>` tags or completely contain the `<head>`. To put this in code, if you're building a site that contains pages accessed by Contribute users, *don't* write your SSIs like this:

```
<!--Code in the head tag -->
</head>
<body>
<!--More code in the body tag -->
```

Instead, write it more like this:

```
<!--Navigation code completely within the body tag -->
```

   EXPLORING KEYWORD SPACE

Keywords are an important part of most any web page. When placed in a `<meta>` tag, keywords help search engines locate the relevant content in your site. Most often folks separate their keywords with commas, like this:

```
<meta name="keywords" content="barbeque, shrimp, recipe">
```

This works great if people are searching by a single keyword; if anyone searches for "barbeque shrimp recipe," however, your page is less likely to come up. If you remove the commas from your keyword and just separate your keywords with spaces, search engines will still pick up all the words individually and as phrases. So, regardless if someone enters "barbeque shrimp" or "shrimp recipe," you'll be cooking.

ZIPPY FORM ORGANIZATION WITH THE <FIELDSET> TAG

One of the keys to good design is proximity: Grouping related elements together makes it easier on the eye and the brain, especially when it comes to lengthy forms. The `<fieldset>` tag is a handy tool to keep in any form designer's palette. Supported by most modern browsers (Internet Explorer 5.0 and later and Netscape Navigator 6.0 and above), the

```
Killer Demo - Microsoft Internet Explorer provided by AT&T Worl...
File   Edit   View   Favorites   Tools   Help
Address   D:\Projects\KillerTips\TMP99rf1k5cxm.htm         Go

  Shipping Address
 Street |

 City    |

 State  |              Zip |

Done                                    My Computer
```

`<fieldset>` tag groups elements by drawing a thin-lined box around them all and adding a legend in the top-left corner of the box. Address info—such as Street, City, State, Zip—is a likely target for a `<fieldset>` tag. It's a cool look and easy to do—you can even use it to provide additional help text. To group existing form elements, go into Code view and select all the desired form elements. (When I've tried to do this in Design view, I've found that Dreamweaver didn't always get all the necessary tags.) Then, from the Forms category of the Insert bar, choose the Fieldset object; you can either click it or drop it on the selection, and a small dialog prompts you for the fieldset legend. Both a `<fieldset>` and a `<legend>` tags are inserted, like this:

```
<fieldset>
<legend>Shipping Address</legend>
<label>Street<input type="text" name="street"></label>
<label>Cty<input type="text" name="city"></label>
<label>Sate<input type="text" name="state"></label>
<label>Zip<input type="text" name="zip"></label>
</fieldset>
```

The legend appears in Design view, but the box outline doesn't. Browser support does vary, so be sure to preview in your favorite browser to see the results. Truly zippy.

   ## WHERE, OH, WHERE HAVE MY WINDOW SIZES GONE?

If the key to being a successful real estate developer is location, location, location; for web-site developers, it's testing, testing, testing. One of the wide-ranging variances that design-ers face are different browser window sizes; you really don't know whether your audience is looking at your site with a window set at 640×480, 800×600, 1024×768, or something high-er. Dreamweaver makes it easy to view your page in different dimensions by choosing the Window Size pop-up on the status bar. It's a pretty nifty feature—sometimes, however, you'll try to use it and none of the options in the list are active. In Windows, Dreamweaver automatically disables the feature whenever your Document window is maximized. To restore the options, back off the maximized state by selecting the Restore Down button on Windows systems.

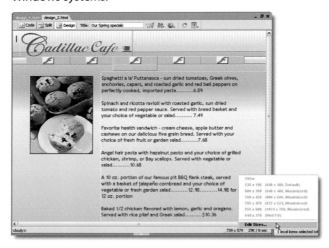

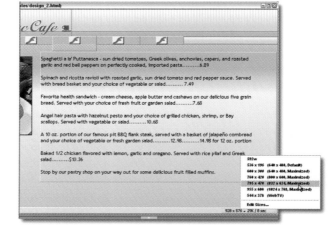

DREAMWEAVER ICONS

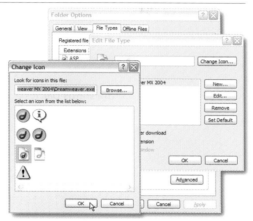

It's been known to happen, another program install overtakes file associations, and uninstalling that program doesn't restore the icons associated with the file type. Search high and low throughout the OS and you won't find any Dreamweaver icon (.ico) files. If you're computer savvy, you might start digging around .dll files in hopes to find them. No such luck there either, I'm afraid. All of Dreamweaver's file icons are stored inside of Dreamweaver.exe.

To change a file's associated icon, from Windows Explorer choose Tools > Folder Options. Click the File Types tab, and then click the file type in the list. Near the bottom of the dialog, you should see an Advanced button that you will click to get to the next dialog. In the Edit File type dialog, you'll see a Change button near the top that you will use to browse to the Dreamweaver.exe file on your system. Then all that's left is to select the icon in the Change Icon dialog and click OK.

PAGING MR. FIND. PAGING MS. REPLACE. YOUR SELECTION IS READY

Don't you just hate it when you have to open up another editor just to do one thing that you can't do in Dreamweaver? Now there's one less reason to fire up those other programs: Find and Replace in a selection. Searching for the references to FooBar Soda in one particular `<div>`? Select that `<div>` from the tag selector and choose Edit > Find and Replace or use that memorable keyboard shortcut, Ctrl+F (Cmd+F). Now here's where the road divides and what happens next depends on what you actually selected. If your selection is under a certain size (512 characters to be exact), the selection is automatically inserted in the Find area; if the number of characters selected is over the magic number, the Find area is left blank. Should the Find area include your selection and you plan to limit your search to the highlighted area — before you do anything else—enter your new search criteria. This will replace the text in the Find area with whatever it is you're looking for. After your new search criteria is in, choose Selected Text from the Find In list at the top of the dialog. Now you're ready to continue with your Find and Replace mission—in a selected area, of course.

  SUPPORT FORUMS AND NEWSGROUPS

Macromedia has set up online forums for user-to-user discussion for all their products including Dreamweaver. You'll find plenty of experts there willing to help you out, including Team Macromedia members (http://www.macromedia.com/go/team). You'll even find us (Joe and Angela) participating from time to time. Choose Help > Macromedia Online Forums to access a page that lists all available forums.

You're probably familiar with web-based forums in general, but you may not have tried NNTP forums, which enable you to view threads in your news reader, such as Outlook Express and Netscape Communicator (http://www.macromedia.com/support/forums/news/). We prefer the newsgroup method because it is much quicker and far more convenient. Careful, though—spending time in the newsgroups can be quite an addiction!

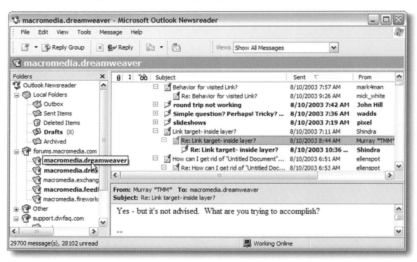

   ## STAYING IN GOOD FORM

Naming conventions are extremely helpful in avoiding common form-processing errors. The trick is to create unique labels for form elements that are instantly identifiable to the developer. My technique is to combine the type of form element with its purpose. For example, I would call a text field for accepting the name of a country `countryText`—whereas a list element for the same purpose would be `countryList`. I use mixed case (also known as *intercapping*) to avoid spaces—a definite no-no in web naming—but this helps keep it legible. Doesn't feel right? Try my partner's method of putting the type of field first, like `txtCountry` or `lstCountry`. Doesn't matter which road you take—the main thing is to pick a direction and stick with it. Both ways will hasten your coding journeys.

   ## GOOGLE ARCHIVES

If you read "Support Forums and Newsgroups" also in this chapter, you're well aware that you can get user-to-user support online 24 hours a day, 7 days a week. Why wait for a response to a question that may have already been asked over the past few years? You don't have to wait; Google has archives of the Dreamweaver (and other Macromedia) forums. Visit http://groups.google.com and click the Advanced Groups Search hyperlink. Enter your search criteria, and in the Newsgroup field enter **macromedia.dreamweaver**. If you want a list of all archived newsgroups, do not enter any search criteria and just enter **macromedia** without **.dreamweaver**. Often this is the quickest way to get answers to your burning Dreamweaver questions.

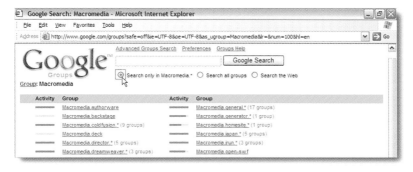

     FANCY-SCHMANCY FORM BUTTONS

Looking to spice up a boring form? A common element to all forms is the Submit button—
and its standard appearance is definitely commonplace. You can replace the ordinary gray
button with a graphic button in one of two ways. If your form has only a Submit button,
with no reset or other type of button, you can use an image field. You can add an input
image using the Image Field object found in the Forms category of the Insert bar. When
users select an image field (that's inside a form), the form is automatically submitted. There
is a drawback to using image fields—you can't use them for other purposes, such as resetting a form. The second method uses JavaScript. In this technique, you bring in a regular
image to act as your Submit button and give it a link like this:
`javascript:document.form1.submit()`, assuming that your form is named `form1`. If
you want to use another graphic to clear a form, just change the link to
`javascript:document.form1.reset()`. Not only do these types of buttons display
the pointing-hand icon, but you could also include rollover images if you like.

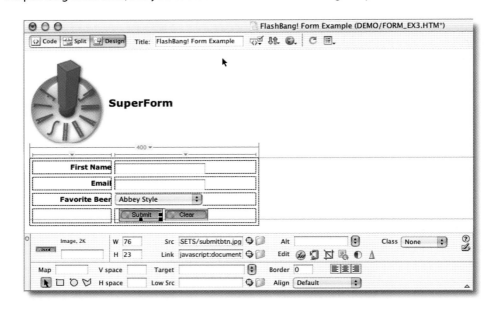

LABEL-LICIOUS

Accessibility seems like such a dry but necessary topic. "Eat your accessibility, Johnny—it's good for you!" But the form element accessibility options, which can be enabled in Preferences, include a rather cool feature: labels. Supported in the latest browsers, the <label> tag makes it easy to associate any form element with specific text, which appears normally but can also be noted by screen

readers. The Input Tag Accessibility Attributes dialog gives you two possible routes to take when creating labels. So what's the proper one to use when? Use the Wrap with Label Tag when your form element and label are side by side; this gives you code like this:

```
<label>First Name<input type="text" name="firstnameText"></label>
```

If you prefer to separate the label and form element into separate table columns, use the Attach Label Tag Using 'for' Attribute option. This choice results in code like this:

```
<label for="firstnameText">First Name</label>
<input type="text" name="firstnameText" id="firstnameText">
```

   BUTTON, BUTTON, WHO'S GOT THE BUTTON?

Why use form buttons just for submitting or resetting forms when they can be pressed into a multitude of services? If you need an instantly recognizable button to trigger any function, the form button is ideal; you don't even need to put it within a <form> tag. The easiest way to assign a function directly to a button is to use the Quick Tag Editor. Select the button and press Ctrl+T (Command+T) to display the <input> tag. Tab to the end of the tag and enter onClick="doMyFunction()" where doMyFunction() is the name of…well, your custom JavaScript function. For simple JavaScript commands such as alerts, you can enter the JavaScript directly, like this:

```
onClick="javascript:alert('Call 555-1234 for help.')"
```

   HITTING THE FARAWAY LINKS

I always thought putting in an absolute URL is a good way to judge your pain threshold. Pretty much anyone can stand to type in your basic domain name in the Link field of the Property inspector, as follows:

```
http://www.pinkparsnips.com/
```

(Listen, it's getting really hard to come up with fictitious website names, so give me a break.)

No problem, right? So then you have to go a little deeper into the site:

```
http://www.pinkparsnips.com/products/pinkparsnip_potstickers/index.php
```

Okay, maybe you're starting to sweat, but you're still holding on. But what if the link is something like this:

```
http://www.pinkparsnips.com/products/pinkparsnip_potstickers/polkadotted/
parabolic/pituitary_perfect/productpage.php
```

Okay, that's it—I can't hold any more in my feeble memory banks. If you're like me, you'd be reaching for that browser, surfing to the page, and copying and pasting the URL. Let me take that pain away, my child. Right from within Dreamweaver, you can create an absolute URL from any page on any server you've defined, in or out of a site. To take advantage of this power, select the Link folder icon as you would normally. When the Select File dialog opens, choose Sites and Servers. In the new dialog, Choose File on Website; a list of all the files on your current remote server displays. To choose from any of your other declared servers or sites, select Websites from the Look In list—the full array is now ready for your double-clicking pleasure. Drill as deep as you like into any one of them and select a file; click OK and the absolute URL is in your doc and not your head. Of course, you'll need to be online to take advantage of this, but is that too small a price to pay to preserve what's left of your brain cells?

  PARLEZ VOUS GEEK?

As the world continues to shrink (don't panic, I'm talking metaphor here), web developers increasingly find they're working with numerous languages and cultures. Dreamweaver offers full Unicode support, which makes creating multilingual web pages so much easier. Another way that Dreamweaver can help is by ensuring the pages are spell-checked. I don't know what the Portuguese word for "typo" is, but I'm sure it puts as much ovo on your face in that language as in any other. Did you know that Dreamweaver includes 14 different spelling dictionaries—everything

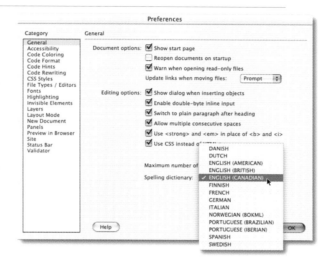

from Danish to Swedish, with 3 flavors of English (American, British, and Canadian) thrown in. To check your page under a different language, open Preferences and, from the General category, pick your choice from the Spelling Dictionary list. The next time you run Text > Check Spelling, you'll be doing your bit to eradikate … err … eradicate typos around the globe.

   HIDDEN GAME

Hidden deep within the Dreamweaver interface is a fun little game you can play when your boss isn't looking. Careful though—it is rather addictive. Select Commands > Create Web Photo Album. When the dialog appears, type **play a game** in the Photo Album Title field. Press Enter (Return) or click OK and the Game dialog will appear. If you're familiar with this color-guessing game, have at it; otherwise, click the Help button to view directions. I've solved the game in only two guesses at my best, but I wasn't really trying … so good luck!

 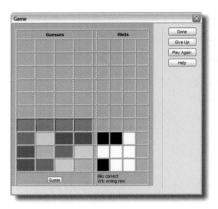

   JAVASCRIPT REQUIRED

You never know when users have fiddled with their browser settings and decided to disable JavaScript. The `<noscript>` tag will let you present those users with a special message only for them. Switch to the HTML category of the Insert bar and then click in the body of the document where you want the message to display—near the top is usually a good spot so that it is seen the moment the page is loaded. Click the No Script icon and the Tag Editor dialog will appear. If you've never used the `<noscript>` tag, you

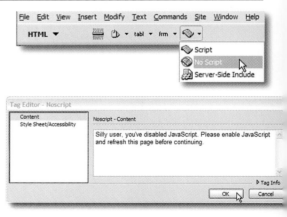

may want to click Tag Info in the lower right of the dialog to display a description and example of the `<noscript>` tag. Enter your message in the text area and if you'd like, switch to the Style Sheet/Accessibility category on the left, fill out the values on the right, and then click OK.

     ## BYE, BYE HELPER TEXT

Sometimes it is necessary to have a form field already filled out so that users understand what they are supposed to enter. The only problem with this method is that it means the users have to delete the prefilled entry themselves, which can be annoying—especially if there are many fields to clear. You can make it easier by clearing the text for them with some easy JavaScript. To clear an `<input>` tag's value, add the following: `onfocus="this.value=''"`. You wouldn't want to clear the form every time the user clicks inside it because that could really get annoying. Let's clear the field only if the default value specified by the value attribute of the `<input>` tag is present, by using this code instead:

```
onfocus="if(this.value==this.defaultValue)this.value=''"
```

You can add the code directly in Code view or take advantage of "Power Event Planning" in Chapter 10.

   AUTOCOMPLETE FORMS

Assuming the user hasn't tweaked his browser settings, AutoComplete for single-line text fields is turned on by default in Internet Explorer. You can disable this feature on a textfield or the entire form if so desired by adding `autocomplete="off"` to either the `<form>` tag or on a case-by-case basis in `<input>` tags. The perfect place to do this in Dreamweaver is in the Attribute tab of the Tag inspector. At the bottom of the Property sheet, just add the `autocomplete` attribute on the left, and the `off` value on the right.

On the other hand, if want to take advantage of AutoComplete—as long as it is enabled—you can add the `vcard_name` attribute with one of several schema names. You can find a list of those schema names with examples at:http://msdn.microsoft.com/workshop/author/forms/autocomplete_ovr.asp

     TRANSFERRING SITES

Do you have a client or co-worker using Dreamweaver? You can save them the time of defining a site by exporting your site definition for them to import. This very method is how you'll transfer sites between your own computers. Select Site > Manage Sites, and then click the site you want to export. Click the Export button and continue with the export—I'm sure you can figure it out. Do the same for each site definition—it is good to have a backup of all site definitions, just in case. In fact, set this book down—but keep it open, of course—and export all of your defined sites right now. It is a known issue that without rhyme or reason, the site definitions may be lost completely. It is important to realize that the .ste files store all the info in the Site Definition dialog box, but it does not back up the files on your site. You need to do that manually. If you opted to include the password in the .ste file, be aware that although it is encrypted, it is conceivable that it can be deciphered. Give the .ste files to your client or co-worker so that they can use the Import button on the Edit Sites dialog box to import the site definition.

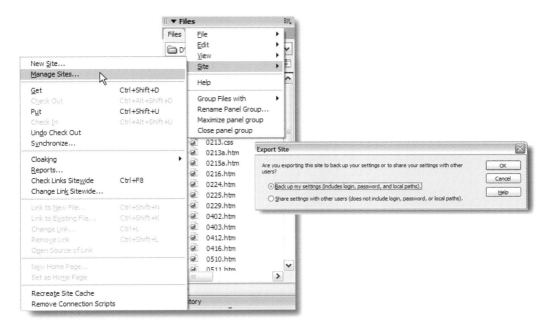

 GETTING GRAPHIC

Dreamweaver has had a long and successful partnership with its sister program, Fireworks. With the latest version, that partnership has reached new heights, even though Fireworks is even more behind the scenes. Since early on, you could optimize a Dreamweaver image with Fireworks—rescaling, reducing the file size, even changing the file format—but it was always within an external process. Now you have the additional ability to crop, resample, alter the contrast, or sharpen your images, right within Dreamweaver. These new tools make short work of fine-tuning a graphic.

The keys to this new graphics power lie right on the Property inspector. Select any JPEG or GIF image and you'll notice a new line-up of icons on the right side. But as another webhead said, "With great power comes great responsibility." Each of the tools alters the embedded image's file. When you crop an image, for example, the dimensions are permanently modified—another reason to always have a backup of your site handy.

One of the icons is not immediately available. Until you resize an image in Dreamweaver either by dragging out the sizing handles or changing the values in the Width and Height fields, the Resample tool is inactive. The Brightness/Contrast and Sharpen tools provide an onscreen preview so that you can max out your graphics in style.

FLASHPAPER SHAZAM!

Ready for another round of good news, bad news? The bad news is that you need
Contribute 2 on your machine to administer Contribute sites with Dreamweaver MX 2004.
The good news is that when you install Contribute 2, you also get the extremely nifty
FlashPaper utility (if you're a Windows user). In case you haven't seen it, FlashPaper converts
any document you can print into a .swf movie, with its own built-in navigation and zoom
controls. Contribute users have a special menu option (Insert > Document as FlashPaper),
but Dreamweaver users have to travel another route. Well, actually two—you can either
drag and drop a printable document on the FlashPaper icon sitting prettily on your
Desktop, or you can print the .swf from the document's application. Yes, you read that right;
I said "print." FlashPaper is, at its heart, a printer driver and automatically available to any
such enabled application. Suppose, for example, you've got a PowerPoint presentation you
want to webify. Power up PowerPoint, load in the preso, click File > Print, select FlashPaper
and presto! When the doc is converted, you'll be prompted for a location to store the brand-
new .swf file. Put it anywhere in your site and then, from Dreamweaver, use Insert > Media >
Flash to bring it into your page.

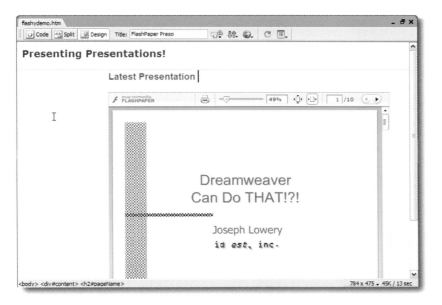

      ## SEE YOUR WAY TO SITELESS EDITING

Since time immemorial (that is, around 1998), Dreamweaver designers have begun their work by defining sites. Before you could do anything, you needed to set up a folder on your system or network for the local site and fill out the remote site info. It's a great system if you're working on a site from the ground up, but what if you just need to go into an existing site, make a quick correction, and get out? Do you still have to do the site dance?

Not no more, not no how. Dreamweaver MX 2004 introduces siteless editing (supply your own fanfare). Now, if you've got the proper connection info, you can set up a server for immediate access. Once connected, grab any available—that is, not checked out—file from the Files panel. Dreamweaver downloads the file and all the graphics and other dependent files. You make your change, save, and put the file back on the server. You're in, you're working, you're out!

To go siteless, first select Site > Manage Sites to open the site management dialog. Then choose New and select FTP & RDS Server from the drop-down list. The first time you perform this operation, Dreamweaver pops up a note, informing you of the limitations of working siteless (no site-wide operations—because there's no site, naturally). After OK'ing the message, the Configure Server dialog is displayed, where you give your new connection a memorable label.

Then you have a choice of working with either FTP or RDS from the Access Type drop-down list. Choose one and the dialog displays the appropriate options. You'll need to enter all the usual configuration info, such as FTP host, username, and password for FTP sites; a separate settings dialog is available for RDS. Once the configuration is completed, Dreamweaver automatically connects and shows you a list of available files (within a snazzy pink folder no less).

Très cool, n'est pas? And if you need to modify the settings for a siteless connection, the usual methods (double-clicking the connection name in the drop-down list or choosing Edit from the Manage Sites dialog) work just swell. Now there's no reason for you not to go siteless, you daredevil you.

REUSABLE JAVASCRIPT

Creating external JavaScript files will not only save download time with users, but also will make updating a site less painful for you. Instead of keeping common JavaScript used throughout the site within the page, externalize the code to its own file and attach it to the document(s) that need it. Choose File > New, select JavaScript in the Basic Page category, and then click Create. Just add the JavaScript code to the file without the `<script>` tags. When it comes time to attach the external JavaScript file to a document, go to the Scripts category of the Assets panel. Clicking the filename will reveal the file's code inside the preview area. You can either drag the file by its name into the document or click the Insert button in the lower left of the Assets panel. The `<script>` tag is added to the document with the proper `src` attribute that points to the JavaScript file. Don't forget to add a `type` attribute to the `<script>` tag if you want to be sure your page uses valid (X)HTML.

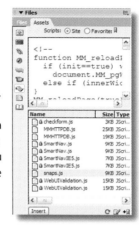

   FOCUS YOUR ATTENTION RIGHT HERE

Here is a simple little JavaScript used to give a specific field focus in a form when the page is loaded so that the user can start filling out the fields right away. Right-click (Ctrl+Click) the `<body>` tag in the tag selector in the lower left of the Document window if you're using Design view and choose Edit tag; or if you're in Code view, get ready to modify the `<body>` tag.

```
Edit tag: <body
          onload="document.theFormName.theFieldName.
          focus();">
```

Here's the code to add to the `<body>` tag:

```
onload="document.theFormName.theFieldName.focus();"
```

Replace `theFormName` with the name of your form and `theFieldName` with the name of the field that you want to have the cursor positioned in when the page loads.

All
Fueled Up

Deadlines, we've all got 'em—even me. Right now I'm thinking, "What the heck can I say about building dynamic applications that is funny for Chapter 8's

All Fueled Up:
The Best of Server-Side

intro?". So I turned to my good friend Dan Short. We were already chatting along when I said, "Tell me something funny about building dynamic sites."

I barely blinked twice before Dan replied, "There are some hidden costs to developing dynamic sites that most people don't think of. You'll need additional equipment such as beer, pizza, thicker glasses, and hair coloring for the gray spots. Once you have these initial supplies in order you'll be ready to dig in."

Of course I replied, "LMAO, I'm stealing this from you for the book with credit <smile />. Is there anything else funny I can permanently borrow from you for the book?"

"Dreamweaver wouldn't be the product it is without Dan... just think about it. Who else would make a blog that yellow? That alone has boosted sales immeasurably, but no one will ever know…" So there you have it folks, Mr. Daniel W. Short's words of wisdom. (For more of Dan's wisdom, see his blog: http://www. dwkillertips.com/go/31) Thanks, Dan!

I know that diving into building dynamically driven sites can be intimidating. You're about to learn all you never knew but were afraid to ask…

   SAFER INCLUDES

One of the beauties of creating dynamic sites is the ability to take advantage of server-side includes. Similar to an external JavaScript file, the code calls the file to be included on a page. When an update is needed, only the single include file needs be updated and uploaded to affect all files that reference it. The biggest mistake you can make using includes is one you may never have considered: your file-naming convention. Many developers like to use an .htm or .inc file extension to help them easily identify the files as an include file. Although it is acceptable to use .inc or .htm as file extensions, if they are found on the server, they could expose server-side code that you would not want users to have access to. Either be certain that these files do not contain server-side code, or use your server language's file extension (.asp, .cfm, .php, and so forth) for the include files. To help you identify the files easily in your site as includes, you may want to put all of your include files in a folder called Includes or name the files with an inc prefix, such as incFooter.asp.

   VIRTUAL OR FILE

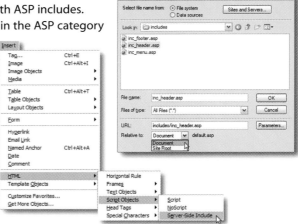

As simple as it is, I still get confused from time to time about when to use virtual or file with ASP includes. Although there's an Include object in the ASP category of the Insert bar, that isn't the best way to go about adding Server-Side Includes. That method will just throw you into Code view to fend for yourself.

Instead, try the HTML category for the Server-Side Includes object or use Insert > HTML > Script Objects > Server-Side Includes. Depending on whether you're using document-relative or site root–relative URLs in the Select File dialog, the right choice, virtual or file, is inserted for the Server-Side Include syntax. Anything that saves me from thinking is a good thing.

     ## PATH TO THE DATABASE

The toughest part of getting started with an ASP site is making the
connection to the database. This is
especially difficult if you don't
know the server's path to the
database file so that you can make
your connection. To keep users
from being able to browse to the
database file on the web, a database should be stored a level
above the root of the site. (If your
host does not allow the database
to be stored above your site's root,
they may provide an alternatively
protected directory that cannot be
browsed from the web.) To get the

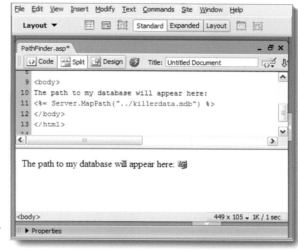

path to the database file, you need to know the name of the folder in which the file is
stored as well as the filename. On any ASP page, somewhere in the code after the `<body>`
tag, add the following:

```
<%= Server.MapPath("..\databaseFolder\theDatabase.mdb") %>
```

You should, of course, replace the part inside the quotation marks with your own information. When you preview the page, you'll get a full path to the file shown in the browser,
which will look something like this:

```
D:\aFolder\wwwroot\yourSite\databaseFolder\theDatabase.mdb.
```

If you don't get the path to your database that way, your host may have disabled "parent
paths," in which case you'd use the following:

```
<%= Server.MapPath(".") %>
```

Then take the path that is returned and adjust it as needed.

   CELLULAR INSURANCE

Insuring your cell phone against loss or theft is a good tip, but instead let's talk about ensuring that table cells have content. You already know that Netscape 4.x can have conniptions
when a cell is left totally empty. You also know that if a table has a border set, empty cells
don't get the border and it looks terrible in Internet Explorer. When you're dealing with a
dynamically driven website, there is often the chance that some of the fields in the database won't return any data. When this happens and there aren't any other contents in a
table cell, you could end up with a totally empty cell if a record is not returned. We can't
have that, now can we? Using an if/else statement, you can determine if a field is not empty
the record should be shown; otherwise, show a non-breaking space or a display message
you've entered—just don't let that cell stay empty. Here's some sample ColdFusion code for
you to chew on:

```
<cfif recordset.theField NEQ "">
<cfoutput>#recordset.theField#</cfouput>
<cfelse> 
</cfif>
```

And sample code for you if you use ASP/VBScript:

```
<% If recordset("theField ") <> "" Then %>
<%= recordset("theField ") %>
<% Else %>
 

<% End If %>
```

You'll find objects in the Insert bar to help you write your if/else statements in a category
for the current document's server model; for example, CFML for .cfm files or ASP for .asp
files.

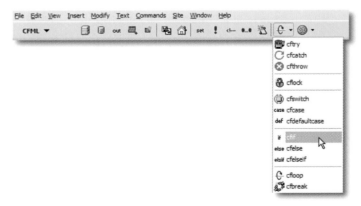

    ONE-CLICK PONY

Remember when Windows operating systems started allowing one-click access and you thought that was so cool? No longer did you have to double-click just right to get a program up and running; just hover and click. But, like many things in computing, every silver lining has a cloud. Ever try to add a dynamic parameter while linking to a new file? You'd think the process would be straightforward: Open dialog, select file, click Parameters, add arguments, close dialogs. But nooooooo. If you've got one-click enabled, the minute you choose a file in the Select File dialog, Dreamweaver (as told to by the OS) thinks you're done, so the file is selected and you have to re-open the dialog to add the parameters. Drives me right up the wall. The way around this problem is backward: When the Select File dialog opens, click that Parameters button first. When you're done adding the arguments, you'll be back in the Select File dialog where you can choose the desired file. Dreamweaver creates the link just as expected, and you have the satisfaction of having brought another OS quirk to its knees.

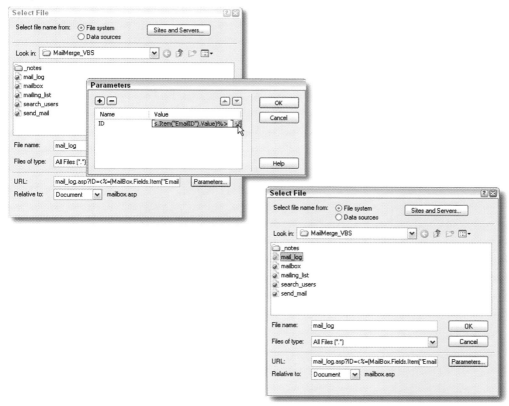

   FORMAT THAT DATA

To get to the all-powerful Format column of the
Bindings panel, you may have to use the horizontal
scrollbar at the bottom of the panel. Yeah, I missed
that too. I adjusted the width of the Format column in
my Bindings panel so that I wouldn't need to scroll by
clicking and dragging the border between the Format
and the Binding column. First you need to select anything that is listed in the Bindings panel in Design
view or insert an item that's listed there in Design
view. Then just click the drop-down arrow in the
Formats column, which will let you choose from a
whole bunch of server formats to pretty up that data.

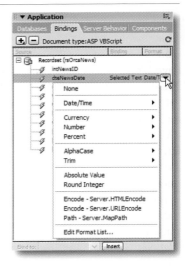

   LOOKING FOR A VIEW

You've mastered all the intricacies of
creating a query—a.k.a. a view—in
Access and you're ready for the rewards
in a Dreamweaver recordset. You've
cleverly joined data from tables called
Conferences and Departments in a view
named ConferenceDepartments. But,
after choosing Recordset from the
Bindings panel and selecting your connection in the Recordset dialog, your
view is not where it should be in the
Table drop-down list. There's
Conferences and there's Departments,
but you won't find
ConferenceDepartments unless you
scroll all the way down the list.
Dreamweaver first alphabetically lists all

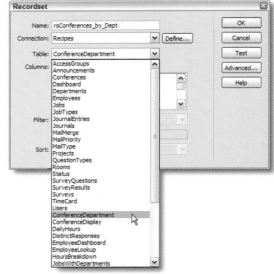

the tables in your data source, followed by all the views. All you hard work is still there, you
just have to dig a little deeper for it.

   ## DUPLICATING RECORDSETS

Make a page, save it as a different page, strip out what you don't need, save again, and continue working. Have you ever done that? I think we all have. Well, if you're going to such lengths just so you don't have to re-create a complicated record-set, don't bother. Just right-click (Ctrl+Click) the recordset and select Copy; then right-click (Ctrl+Click) again in either the Server Behavior or Bindings panel and select Paste. You can paste in a new document's Server Behaviors or Bindings panel, but if you paste the recordset you copied in the same document, Dreamweaver gives the recordset a new name. If you're pasting to the same document, I assume it is because you're going to modify that recordset; you shouldn't ever need the same exact recordset twice. ColdFusion users enjoy being able to use a field as many times as they like, but if you're using

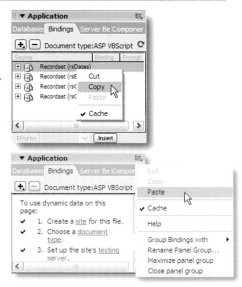

ASP and have emptied a recordset, you may be tempted to define an identical one. Don't give in to that temptation; just add `<% rsMyRecordsetNameHere.MoveFirst() %>` to the page before the second usage of the recordset and that will get you back to the start of your recordset again.

   ## YES, WE HAVE NO RECORDS TODAY

A results page for the standard search applica-tion is generally set up to handle any number of items—some even use recordset naviga-tion so that users can page through the results. However, what if there are no matches

to the search criteria? Do you really want a "Now showing 0 of 0 records" message on the screen? Of course you don't! You want something kind, but firm, like, "No matches. Try again. Loser." With the use of two standard server behaviors, you can hide unnecessary elements and simultaneously show your message. To hide your recordset navigation (and anything else unwanted), select the undesired elements and apply the Show If Recordset Not Empty server behavior. This shows the region only if some results are found and otherwise it's hid-den. Next, add your "No Records Found" message (or a Flash sound file that gives 'em the raspberry), select it, and then apply Show If Recordset Is Empty. Presto-chango—two com-pletely different looks to handle any search outcome.

   REUSING MEMO FIELDS

With ColdFusion, you can use a field as many times as you want for display or for if statements; it doesn't matter. On the other hand, ASP is a little more finicky when it comes to
reusing memo-type fields. Suppose that you want to check to see whether a memo-type
field in the database is empty, and if it is, you want to display a message to the user. Then
later on the same page you want to put the same memo field in another location. You're
gonna get errors, bubba, or no data—depending on what you're trying to do. When you
need to reuse a memo field, the way to get it working is to assign the memo field's value to
a variable, and then call that variable whenever you need it. Take this, for example:

```
<% Dim myMemoFieldVariable
myMemoFieldVariable =
➥rsMyRecordset.Fields.Item("memMyActualMemoField").value
%>
```

Now whenever you need to display the variable, do so like this:

```
<%= myMemoFieldVariable %>
```

Remember that you must declare the variable before you try to use it in the page, or it
won't work!

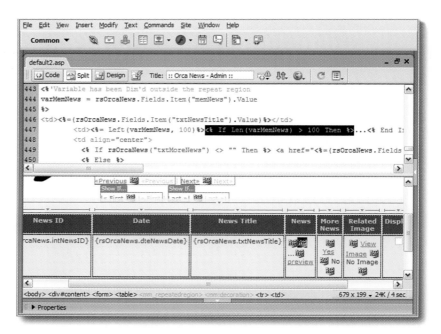

    DYNAMIC ALTERATIONS

Alternating table row colors sure does make it easier on the eyes to locate data in large tables. After you've created your dynamic table, it just takes a tiny bit of hand-coding to create this common effect. Note that we have two custom classes, one named `altRowColor` and the other `altRowColor2`. Feel free to use your own class names in their place; just be sure you've defined the classes in your CSS.

In ColdFusion, it is super easy; just add a class attribute with the ColdFusion code shown here to the `<tr>` tag that is created dynamically:

```
class=#IIF(CurrentRow MOD 2, DE('altRowColor'), DE('altRowColor2'))#"
```

In ASP VBScript, it is a little more complicated. You need to declare a variable and determine its value before calling it in the `<tr>` tag. Just inside the start of your Repeat Region, add the following:

```
<%
Dim altColor
If Repeat1__numRows Mod 2 Then
altColor = "altRowColor"
Else
altColor = " altRowColor2"
End If
%>
```

I used `Repeat1__numRows` in this example, but if you've more than one Repeat Region applied to the page you'll need to use the correct one. Just look in the While statement that starts the repeated region for the right variable name. Inside the `<tr>` tag, place `class="<%= altColor %>"`. There you have it, dynamically styled table rows.

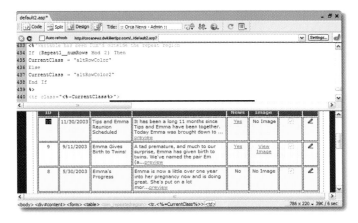

   COPING WITH LOGIN FAILURE

I'm not a big fan of Sorry pages, are you? You know, you attempt to log in to an application and clumsy-finger-itis strikes and you mistype your username or password. Suddenly you're faced with a some variation of an entire HTML page devoted to telling you that you've failed and you should click the Back button to give it another go. Too much work! I've got a easier method.

The beauty of this approach is that it uses the standard Dreamweaver Log In User server behavior and one little bit of extra code. First, apply your Log In User server behavior normally; in the If Log In Fails, Go To field of the dialog, replace the URL to your "I'm sorry" page with an address like this: `login.asp?failed=true`, where `login.asp` (or `login.cfm` or `login.php`) is the current login page. This redisplays the login screen, giving folks a chance to re-enter their info without having to engage the Back button. Next, wherever you'd like your error message to appear to inform the user of the failed login attempt, add ASP code like this:

```
<%If (cStr(Request("failed"))<>"") Then %>
The username or password entered is not valid. Please try again.
<% End If %>
```

The ColdFusion version of this code would look like this:

```
<cfif IsDefined("URL.failed")>
The username or password entered is not valid. Please try again.
</cfif>
```

In PHP the code would read:

```
<?php echo
(isset($_GET['failed']))?"The
username or password entered
is not valid. Please try again"."";
?>
```

Feel free to make your error message as uplifting or disparaging as you like.

OVERCOMING CF LOGIN ERRORS

It is definitely a good idea to password protect pages that should only be accessed by administrators or registered users. Dreamweaver's Login User server behavior for ColdFusion does most of the work for you, but not all of it. If you just apply the server behavior and have not enabled sessions in your Application.cfm file, you'll run into errors because the server behavior depends on sessions. If you don't have an Application.cfm file at the root of your site, create one and insert the following code (at minimum—there are other attributes that you may want to use):

```
<cfapplication name="UpTo64Characters"
sessionmanagement="yes">
```

With the exception of the `<cfsilent>` tag, the `<cfapplication>` tag should be the first tag in your Application.cfm file. Of course the name of the application is up to you. Select Window > Reference and choose the Macromedia CFML Reference to look up more information on the `<cfapplication>` tag and its attributes.

WIZARDING WITHOUT WARLOCKS

Any Doc Strange devotees out there? For those of you not up on your Marvel Golden Age of Comics, Dr. Strange was a wizard given to pro-nouncements like, "By the hoary hosts of Hoggoth!" Well, the good doctor has nothing on our own weaver of dreams—especially when it comes to quickly creating both the front end and the back end of two of the most commonly used applications: insert record and update record. Both server behaviors require a form to take in new or updated information and both tie the form elements to their equivalents in the data source. Creating the forms with all the elements and then assigning each element to the appropriate data source tips the tedium scale way over—why not use a wizard to handle both chores at once? Check out Insert > Application Objects > Insert Record > Record Insertion Form Wizard and its good brother Insert > Application Objects > Update Record > Record Update Form Wizard. You don't even have to put in a form tag; Dreamweaver does it all. Before you know it, you'll be banishing the dread Dormammu to the mystic realm as well as completing your applications in record time.

   ROLLOVER, FIDO1; ROLLOVER, FIDO2

Although it's most common to see text fields be a part of a repeat region, you can, of course, include images. Many result pages from a catalog search include both a text and visual description of the items sought after. Now, let's say you want to get really fancy and add rollover effects to those images. Sounds simple enough, right? You just assign a Swap Image behavior and specify a data field from your recordset as the src attribute for the second image. Unfortunately, the Swap Image behavior won't work without tweaking the image name (not the src) to make it unique for every item. Here's what the original rollover code looks like:

```
<a href="javascript:;" onmouseout="MM_swapImgRestore()"
onmouseover="MM_swapImage('Image1','',
➥'<%=(rsCat.Fields.Item("imageover").Value)%>',0)">
<img name="Image1" border="0"
src="<%=(rsCat.Fields.Item("image").Value)%>">
```

To get a rollover to work, you'll need to append an incrementing variable to the name attributes so that each image in the repeat region is unique, like this ASP code (the added code is in bold):

```
<a href="javascript:;" onmouseout="MM_swapImgRestore()"
onmouseover="MM_swapImage('Image<%=Repeat1__numRows%>','',
➥'<%=(rsCat.Fields.Item("imageover").Value)%>',0)">
<img name="Image<%=Repeat1__numRows%>" border="0"
src="<%=(rsCat.Fields.Item("image").Value)%>">
```

ColdFusion users can use the #CurrentRow# attribute to get the same effect.

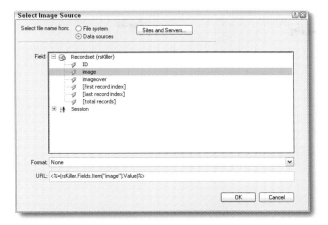

```
Untitled Document (kt/DynamicRollover.asp*)
60 <%
61 While ((Repeat1__numRows <> 0) AND (NOT rsKiller.EOF))
62 %>
63
64 <a href="#" onMouseOut="MM_swapImgRestore()" onMouseOver=
   "MM_swapImage('dynoRollover','','<%=(rsKiller.Fields.Item(
   "imageover").Value)%>',1)"><img name="dynoRollover" border="0"
   src="<%=(rsKiller.Fields.Item("image").Value)%>"></a>
65 <br>
66
```

```
Untitled Document (kt/DynamicRollover.asp*)
60 <%
61 While ((Repeat1__numRows <> 0) AND (NOT rsKiller.EOF))
62 %>
63
64 <a href="#" onMouseOut="MM_swapImgRestore()" onMouseOver=
   "MM_swapImage('dynoRollover<%=Repeat1__numRows%>','','<%=(
   rsKiller.Fields.Item("imageover").Value)%>',1)"><img name=
   "dynoRollover<%=Repeat1__numRows%>" border="0" src="<%=(
   rsKiller.Fields.Item("image").Value)%>"></a>
65 <br>
66
```

CHAPTER 8 · The Best of Server-Side   **173**

  POWER EVENT PLANNING

Looking for a way to trigger a custom JavaScript or server function? The Behaviors panel is open for business! Not only does it enable you to choose any of the Dreamweaver built-in JavaScript behaviors, you can also enter your own function for any recognized event. Here's how it works: Select the tag you want to trigger the behavior and switch to the Behaviors panel by choosing Window > Behaviors (or that ever-popular Shift+F3 keyboard shortcut). The Behaviors panel lets you see either just the events and behaviors already applied or all the possible

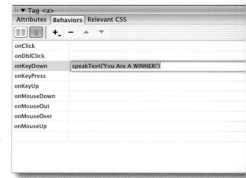

events for the selected tag—choose the View option from the two buttons on the left of the panel. Either way, choose your event from the column on the left and enter the JavaScript or dynamic code in the column on the right. Dreamweaver writes both event and behavior directly into the tag. If your code requires quotes, use single quotes rather than double quotes—Dreamweaver converts double quotes to the character entity (`&quot;`)—a no-no in those browser social circles.

   FORM-AL TESTING

Live Data view is good not only for testing URL parameters, but also for checking form-encoded values. As I'm sure you remember from HTML Forms 101, a form using the GET method passes the values via the URL parameter, whereas a POST method form sends the info in the body of the message sent to the server. You've seen how the URL parameter field works—to test values for a POST form,

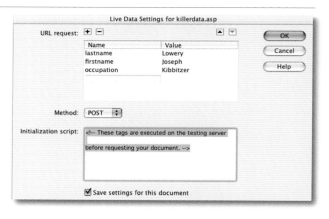

select Live Data Settings from the Live Data toolbar and enter the needed name/value pairs. The names will correspond to the form field names, and the values are what the user enters or selects. Be sure to change the Method to POST. This will hide the unneeded URL parameter field; to get it back, change the Method to GET.

GETTING IT RIGHT FROM THE DATA SOURCE

Creating data-driven pages is like coming down a ladder—miss that first step and you're in for an unwelcome surprise. A data-driven page really starts with the proper formulation of the data itself. Let's look at three areas often misunderstood by web application newbies who are dealing with text, links, and images. First, text is far more flexible in databases than is commonly assumed. For example, a memo field in Access (used when the data runs longer than 255 characters) also can hold HTML tags; so you could store—and retrieve— multiple paragraphs with full formatting. When working with data that will be included as links, you might be tempted to set the data field to a hyperlink type. Hyperlink-styled data looks real pretty in Access but is completely useless in Dreamweaver; store your linking data as straight text instead. With images, it's best just to save just the filename and not the path to the image. If you want to include dynamic images located in a separate folder, choose Insert > Image, and then choose the Select File Name from Data Source option. Select the proper field and, in the URL field, prepend the desired path (in human words, add the path before the code). For example, an ASP final URL might resemble this code:

```
images/thumbs/<%=(employees.Fields.Item("images").Value)%>
```

The ColdFusion code is different, even though the concept remains the same:

```
images/thumbs/<cfoutput>#employees.images#</cfoutput>
```

Same deal with PHP:

```
images/thumbs/<?phpecho
$row_employees['images'];?>
```

  NOW THAT'S REFRESHING

So you're working in Live Data view, enjoying the fact that Dreamweaver lets you design your page with actual data shown, and you change the color of one of the dynamic text fields—but none of the other data in the repeat region changes. What's up with that? You've got Auto-Refresh enabled: Why doesn't it automatically refresh? The Auto-Refresh option only updates the page when a change is made server side—and text color changes (whether via HTML or CSS) are definitely client side. To propagate a client-side change, select the Refresh icon on the Live Data toolbar. To see the Auto-Refresh option in action, change the format of a selected dynamic text element from the Format column of the Bindings panel. You could, for example, specify the AlphaCase to be Upper and all the dynamic text entries would display in uppercase after Dreamweaver detects the format change and automatically refreshes the page.

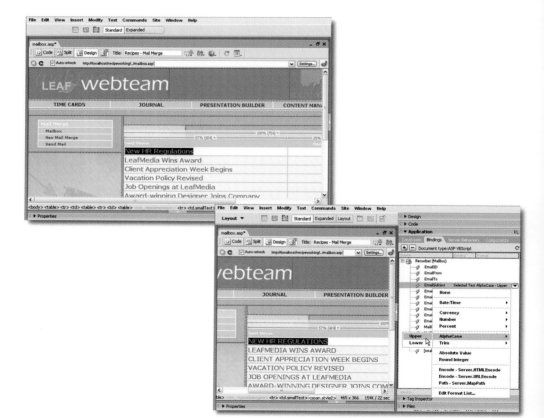

   ## CUSTOM RECORDSET NAVBAR

When you are building a page that displays a lot of data-driven entries, recordset navigation is often essential. When you use recordset navigation, Dreamweaver provides almost instant gratification. Choose the Insert > Application Objects > Recordset Navigation Bar, and Dreamweaver provides a complete navigation aid. In addition to inserting eight separate server behaviors, Dreamweaver adds either text or images to create links to the next, previous, first, and last set of records. Naturally, you can style the text however you like, but what if you'd prefer to use custom images instead of the Macromedia-inserted ones? If you're using the Recordset Navigation Bar throughout your site, replace the source images found in the Dreamweaver MX 2004\Configuration\Shared\UltraDev\Images folder: first.gif, last.gif, next.gif, and previous.gif. After you replace the source images, Dreamweaver uses your custom images rather than the standard ones. Of course, if you don't want an all-in-one solution, you can replace the images used on a case-by-case basis. Just double-click the graphic to swap in a new image in your local site folder.

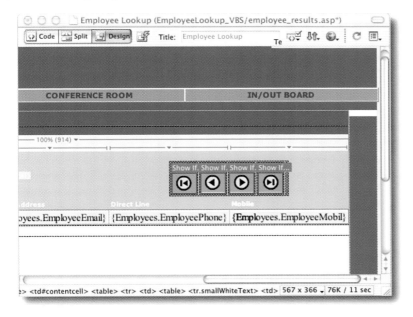

   STOP AND START COLDFUSION SERVER

Why use up precious resources running ColdFusion Server when you're not using it? (This tip is Window's only.) Normally on Windows you need to right-click My Computer and then choose Manage. Next you have to Expand Services and Applications, and then click Services. Finally you have to right-

Start CFMX.cmd
Windows NT Command Script
1 KB

Stop CFMX.cmd
Windows NT Command Script
1 KB

click each of the ColdFusion services listed one by one, and then choose Stop or Start. That just takes way too long for my tastes. Instead I've made two .cmd (Command) files that I use to start and stop ColdFusion server. Create a plain-text file and save it as Start CF Server.cmd with the following content:

```
net start "ColdFusion MX ODBC Agent"
net start "ColdFusion MX ODBC Server"
net start "ColdFusion MX Application Server"
```

Now create another plain-text file and save it as Stop CF Server.cmd with the following contents:

```
net stop "ColdFusion MX Application Server"
net stop "ColdFusion MX ODBC Agent"
net stop "ColdFusion MX ODBC Server"
```

Whenever you want to start or stop ColdFusion MX Server, just double-click the proper .cmd file and you're good to go. Just don't lose those files! I put shortcuts to mine in the Quick Launch bar on my taskbar for easy access.

WIDENING THE .NET

Got some nifty .NET custom tags you want to fold into Dreamweaver? Rev up that folding engine and let's bring 'em in! Dreamweaver is capable of importing both compiled (.dll) and noncompiled (.ascx) tags through the Tag Libraries feature. Start the process by choosing Edit > Tag Libraries and, from the Tag Library Editor, choose Add (+). Under the ASPNET menu, you'll have the option of bringing in all the custom tags found on your testing server or a selected number. Compiled tags need to be stored in the bin directory at the site root, whereas noncompiled ones can be pretty much anywhere. After the tags have

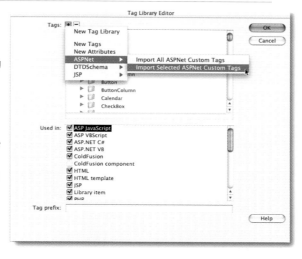

been imported, Dreamweaver code completion and code hints capabilities are enabled for those tags. Now you can stretch that .NET as far as you want.

MULTIPLE APPLICATION.CFM

In case you weren't aware, it's possible to have multiple Application.cfm files in one site. In fact, you could have one Application.cfm for every folder in your site. What good does this do you? When a page is called, the ColdFusion server walks up the directories, looking for the first Application.cfm file it finds. When it finds that first Application.cfm file, it runs all the code located in the file. This means that you could use an Application.cfm file in folder 1 to handle one type of password protection, and use a different Application.cfm file in folder 2 to handle a different password protection. When you start playing, you'll find all kinds of wonderful uses for multiple Application.cfm files.

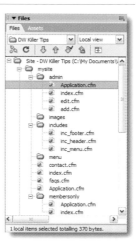

   MAPPING FORM ELEMENTS AND DATA FIELDS

Both the Insert Record and Update Record server behaviors are essential to about half of the web application work I do, which is devoted to administrative chores. Although their use is greatly appreciated, they can be a bit of a chore to set up, especially if you have a lot of fields. You'll find that a great deal of time is spent mapping the form elements on the page to the fields in the data source. Careful planning can complete-

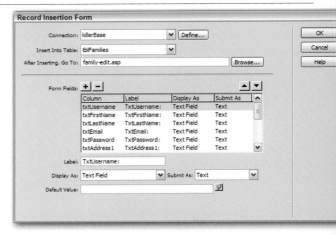

ly eliminate this time-intensive phase. If you name each form element with the same name as its corresponding database field, Dreamweaver will automatically map one to the other when applying either the Insert Record or Update Record server behavior. Moreover, you have a little flexibility because this feature is not case sensitive. The first time you see Dreamweaver complete this task in seconds, you'll agree that it's a beautiful thing.

   TO LOCK OR UNLOCK: THAT IS THE QUESTION

Templates and dynamic applications are a real powerhouse combination. Many web applications are composed of similar, if not the same basic layout where only the dynamic content changes. In Dreamweaver, server-side code can be added to templates outside the `<html>` tags. This functionality is really super because it means changes can be made easily to both the server and static page elements; you could, for example, add a Restrict Access to Page server behavior to a template and instantly protect a full slate of pages. Dreamweaver also offers another degree of control of which you may not be aware: the area outside the `<html>` tags can be locked or editable, just like a region on the page. By default, this external area is unlocked, which allows server-side code to be added to any documents derived from a template. To lock the region, add this code in the `<head>` area:

```
<!-- TemplateInfo codeOutsideHTMLIsLocked="true" -->
```

After saving your template and updating the associated pages, template instances will no longer be able to add or edit server-side code that is written outside the `<html>` tags.

SOPHISTICATED CFMAIL

Don't be fooled by the attribute descriptions for the `<cfmail>` tag in the Macromedia
CFML Reference in the Reference panel (Window > Reference), Contrary to the descriptions,
you aren't limited to just an email address for the fields that require them. You can provide a
name and an email address in the following format:

```
Your Name <you@youremail.com>
```

If you use the Tag Chooser or the cfmail object to insert your `<cfmail>` tag, you'll get the
Tag Editor dialog. If you add this syntax through the dialog, Dreamweaver incorrectly
encodes the < and > symbols unless you uncheck the Special Characters check box in the
Code Rewriting section of Edit > Preferences. Personally, I think this tag is best hand-coded
in Dreamweaver. Here's a sample tag that you can try out if you want:

```
<cfmail
to="Bill Gates <billy@microsoft.com>"
from="Anonymous <spam@microsoft.com>"
subject="CFMAIL kicks CDO's backside"
>
ColdFusion is better than ASP, Neener, neener, neener! :-p
</cfmail>
```

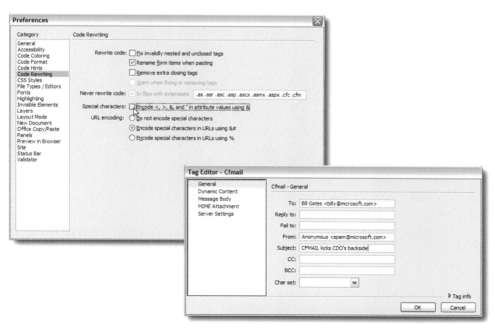

  I'D GO OFFLINE, IF ONLY I HAD THE CACHE

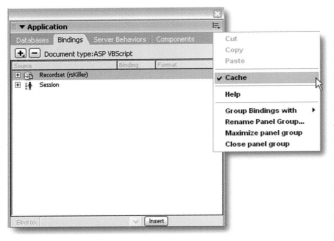

Don't always have a data source connection? Fear not! You can continue working, you lucky dog, as long as your cache is enabled. You probably didn't realize it, but to speed up development of web applications, Dreamweaver caches recordsets and other dynamic content, such as session variables and JavaBeans. This means that if you drop your data source connection for whatever reason, you can still apply the dynamic content to the page by dragging elements from the Bindings panel or inserting a server behavior. To make sure that the cache is up and running, choose the Options menu from the Bindings panel; by default, the Cache option is checked.

Unfortunately, the cache is not all powerful—you won't be able to modify the existing recordsets, add new ones, or enter into Live Data view without an active data source connection. But then, you know what they say, "Cache isn't everything."

   SELECT ONE, SELECT 'EM ALL

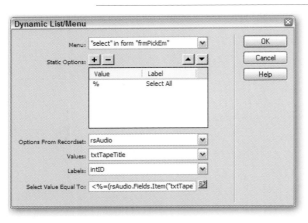

When working with lists/menu form elements, you have an option to enable multiple selections. Well, I'll see your multiple select and raise you a "Select All." You can very easily add a list option that selects any entry—a very helpful feature when creating search pages. To create such an option, choose your list and then, from the Property inspector, choose Dynamic. In the Dynamic List/Menu dialog box, add a new entry to the static list by selecting Add (+). Enter any desired label, such as Select All, and under the Value column enter a percent sign, **%**. The percent sign serves as a wildcard and makes any data value valid.

    ## COLDFUSION DSN VARIABLES

After you've created your Data Source Name (DSN) in ColdFusion Administrator and gone through all the steps in the Bindings panel, you're ready to start creating recordsets. Every time you create a `<cfquery>`, you provide the DSN and a username and password if one is required. If you prefer to hand-code your `<cfquery>` tags, you have to remember what you called the DSN, the username, and the password. Typos happen; things break. Inevitably something happens and you have to change your DSN information. Now you have to go through the entire site making sure to change all instances. Then you have to upload all affected files. You can avoid this mess by using variables for DSN information in your Application.cfm. If you always use the same variable-naming convention for every site you build, it will make things even easier for you. Here's my usual with placeholder values:

```
<cfset request.theDSN = "dsn_goes_here">
<cfset request.theUser = "username_goes_here">
<cfset request.thePass = "password_goes_here">
```

For Dreamweaver to recognize these variables, you need to register them in the Bindings panel. Click the (+) button in the Bindings panel and then choose Data Source Name Variable. In the Variable name field, type **request.theDSN**, and then select the corresponding DSN in the Data Source list and Click OK. After you've done this step, you can create recordsets using the variables set in the Application.cfm as shown previously.

If you're using the Recordset dialog, you'll see #request.theDSN# in the Data Source drop-down list. You need to manually enter the username and password if you've set that up. For example, you enter **#request.theUser#** in the User Name field and **#request.thePass#** in the Password field. The resulting code will look something like this:

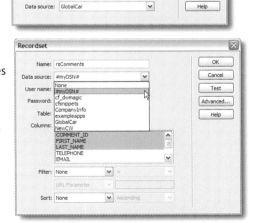

```
<cfquery name="rsRecordsetName" datasource="#request.theDSN#"
username="#request.theUser#" password="#request.thePass#">
```

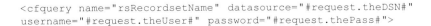

Peel Rubber

Maxing Out Your Code

You're not the hand-coding type or maybe you think that you already know how to hand-code and can afford to skip this chapter. Don't even think

Peel Rubber:
Maxing Out Your Code

about it! In my observations of other developers, I've noticed that there are three kinds of hand-coders. There's the mouse-user extraordinaire who will do practically everything with the mouse and uses the keyboard as little as possible. There are the keyboard geniuses who avoid using the mouse at all costs. (I know one developer who looks like he's making love to his keyboard!) The rest who fall somewhere in-between—folks who quite possibly may not be working as efficiently as they could be because they don't know the ins and outs of doing things with the keyboard or the mouse.

That's what this chapter is all about—working with Code efficiently—while either in Code or Design view. Yes, you can even hand-code while working in Design view. Anyone can hand-code—even the most horrible typists, go figure! Whether you're an experienced hand-coder, or a complete hand-coding virgin you're bound to pick up some super timesaving tips in this chapter. Don't be afraid to get your hands dirty in the code—after all, that's what a good anti-bacterial soap is for, right?

   CODE MANIPULATION MAGIC

Ready to wow your other geeky friends? Or just want to get your detailed code work done a little faster? With the new Code view–only Selection menu, you can do both with the greatest of ease. Just highlight some code, right-click (Ctrl+Click) to get to the context menu and choose Selection. Now you can change the case on your selection up or down or just alter the tag case and leave the content alone. The ability to remove all tags from a selected block of code is also extremely dandy.

   OOPS, BACKSPACE...

You're hand-coding, a code hint pops up, and you make a typo...so, of course, you instinctively press the Backspace key. The only problem is that now you don't get the code hints until you press the Spacebar again. Instead of pressing the Backspace key once, you press it again, and then press the Spacebar so you can move forward once and see the code hints again. Gee, what a pain that is! You needn't go through that anymore. Next time you make a mistake, press Backspace to remove your error, and then press Ctrl+Spacebar (Command+Spacebar) to pop up the Code Hints menu again. Your cursor stays in place; it does not move forward. Now you can take advantage of the code hints provided. This technique works in Code view or the Quick Tag Editor. If you've altered the timing of Code Hints in Preferences, this shortcut can also come in handy to display the hints faster than your Preferences setting.

   ## OBSESSIVE COMPULSIVE CODE FORMATTING

It's rather disgusting how important neat code has become to me. I don't know how I got this bad, but Dreamweaver makes it so easy to be so anal about code formatting that I just can't help myself. Commands > Apply Source Formatting snaps code into place based on the preferences set in Edit > Tag Libraries. Being the keyboard short-cut fanatic that I am, this menu option just wasn't enough for me. Select Edit > Keyboard Shortcuts and assign a key-board shortcut to the Apply Source Formatting command. I happened to choose Ctrl+Shift+Backspace (Command+Shift+Backspace) because it was free. If you're as finicky as I am, you'll even assign a similar shortcut, such as Ctrl+Backspace (Command+Backspace), to the Apply Source Formatting to Selection command.

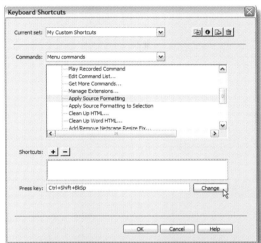

   A CHARACTER IN EVERY CROWD

As if the Insert > HTML > Special Characters > Other 99 characters just aren't enough for you, there is a way to access roughly 255 instead as long as you have Code Hints enabled in Preferences. If you can recognize a character itself or its named entity, you can hand-code it easily in Dreamweaver; you don't even need to know the keyboard shortcuts!

In Code view, type an ampersand (&) and it will bring up the code hints for all "named" special characters (numbered special characters do not have code hints). Then press the next letter in the name until the special character you want is highlighted, and press Enter (Return). Alternatively, you can press the down-arrow key to highlight a named character and then press Enter (Return).

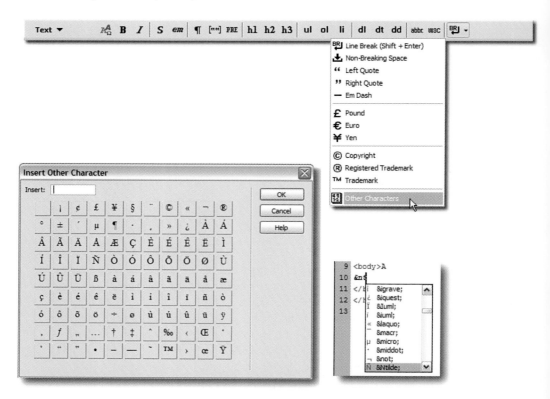

     CODE CHAMELEON

To help you recognize code without thinking much about it, Dreamweaver assigns color and formatting to various types of code. Maybe you're used to another program's style of syntax coloring or perhaps you just prefer to change the formatting to something more readable.

I got used to having JavaScript strings colored in green because that's how Dreamweaver 4 colored them. Ever since then, they've been black by default. If the strings are colored green (#009900), I can instantly see that I've made a mistake when I notice that the code turns black.

To access Code Coloring options, choose Edit > Preferences (Dreamweaver > Preferences) or Ctrl+U (Command+U), and then select Code Coloring from the list that appears on the left. In the Document type list, select HTML and then click Edit Coloring Scheme. This is so cool; you don't even need to know the official name for the syntax you want to customize. Don't select anything in the Styles For list just yet. Scroll down in the Preview area and click the Allaire URL, http://www.allaire.com. Did you see that? JavaScript String is now selected in the Styles For list!

Now that JavaScript String is selected, choose a text color using the color swatch's color picker or type a hexadecimal value (#009900). If you'd like, you can even set a background color and bold, italics, or underlined formatting. After you've made your choices, you'll see that the Allaire URL is now colored. Keep in mind that you've set this only for HTML documents. You need to make the change for each document type in which you intend to use JavaScript. Chances are that you'll want to do this for the JavaScript document type and your server model of choice at the very least. As you can see, code coloring is not limited to JavaScript; the list of options is quite extensive.

    CODE LINE-ING UP TABLES

One of the neatest tricks found in Code view—and I like my neat tricks—is the Convert
Lines to Table option. If you've got a bunch of `<form>` tags that you want to pretty up in a
table, just highlight the mess of them (without grabbing the `<form>` tags themselves),
right-click (Ctrl+Click), and choose Selection > Convert Lines to Table. Presto-table-o, all your
separate lines are in a `<td>` tag. Watch out, however: Be careful not to grab the `<head>` or
`<body>` tags in your selection when issuing this command; Dreamweaver throws those into
the table as well and your page is, shall we say, toast. (Until you Undo, 'natch.)

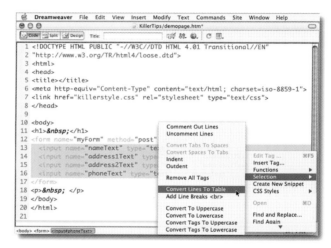

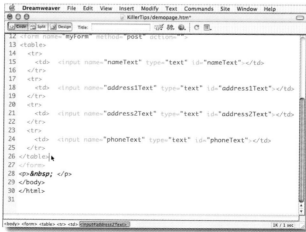

   ## INSTANT GRA-TAG-IFICATION

Want to wow your geeky friends? Want to stun your non-geeky friends into a perpetual "Whaa"? Show them how Dreamweaver can import an entire new DTD or language schema with one command? "Zowie," you say? Then read on, my geek buddy. As I'm sure you know, being the ubergeek you are, when a new XML language or other markup language is crafted, a Document Type Definition (DTD to you and me) is written that specifies the included tags and respective attributes. Dreamweaver has the power to read a DTD and be ready to write code in whatever new language is described. Let's say you want to use Dreamweaver as your new SVG editor, so you go up to the W3C and download the SVG DTD. Then, choose Edit > Tag Libraries in Dreamweaver. Select Add (+) and choose the DTD Schema > Import XML DTD or Schema File option. Browse to your file and before you say Tim Berners-Lee backward, Dreamweaver has imported the file and set up your new tag set. If you want you can even continue to use the Tag Libraries dialog to specify how you want your new tags styled (uppercase, lowercase, indented, you name it) when Dreamweaver puts 'em on the page. What more could any geek want? Besides the latest wrist refrigerator from Sony, I mean.

   GIMME A HINT PLEASE

Code hints and tag completion make hand-coding for a typlexic person like me so much easier. (See http://www.typlexia.com for more info.) So if you thought you were doomed to Design view due to lack of typing skills, you're in for a treat.

If you've never customized the Code Hints category of Preferences before, tag completion and code hints will be already enabled. Tag completion means that after you type the closing angle bracket of the opening tag, the closing tag will be added automatically for you.

Following the opening <body> tag, let's start coding a table. Begin by typing the opening angle bracket, and then type **t**. As soon as you press the key, table is highlighted in the list. Go ahead and press Enter (Return). Now, type a space, and a list of available attributes for the <table> tag displays. Let's add a background color; type **bg** and that highlights the bgcolor attribute we want, so press Enter (Return). Check it out; the Color Picker appeared! Use your arrow keys to maneuver to the color you want to use and then press Enter (Return) or use the mouse to select one. After you select or type the color value, your cursor automatically moves past the bgcolor attribute's closing quotation mark. When you are adding an attribute that doesn't offer a hint for the value, you need to use your right-arrow key to move past the closing quotation mark.

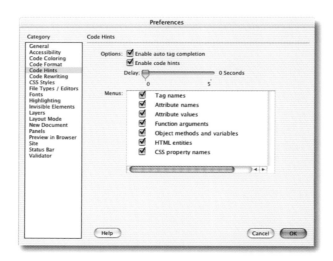

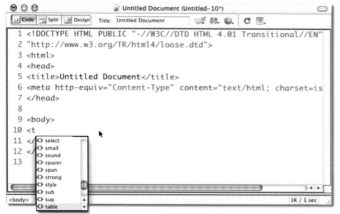

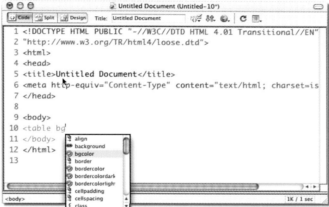

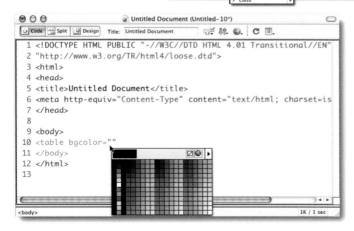

INSERT HTML IN DESIGN VIEW

You're working in Design view—yes, even "real" hand-coders do that sometimes—and you realize that you need to insert an HTML tag, what should you do? You could switch to Code view and do it there, use the Tag Chooser object, or hand-code it from Design view.

Truth be told, all of the options work—and there are actually a few others you'll read about later in this chapter—but the Quick Tag Editor can help you add that tag quickly and easily.

To access the Quick Tag Editor, you could click the pencil icon in the upper-right corner of the Property inspector; choose Insert HTML from the document's context menu; select Quick Tag Editor from the Modify menu; or use the Ctrl+T (Command+T) keyboard shortcut.

When the Quick Tag Editor appears, type the tag and any attributes, and then, without typing the closing tag, press Enter (Return) to return to the document and close the Quick Tag Editor. Dreamweaver adds the closing tag for you. Your cursor is automatically placed between the opening and closing of the tag you just entered. That's what I call convenient.

<a href="default.html">home</a>

    WRAP TAG MODE

Every now and then, there will come a time when you need to wrap a selection with a specific HTML tag. Superscript and subscript are perfect examples of cases in which you might want to use this technique. Let's say that you want to make a trademark symbol

superscript. First, add the trademark symbol (you'll find it in the Text category of the Insert bar in the Characters menu), and then make sure that you have it selected in Design view. Now press Ctrl+T (Command+T) and the Quick Tag Editor appears in Wrap Tag mode. (If the Quick Tag Editor appears in a different mode, press the keyboard shortcut again until it displays that it is in Wrap Tag mode.) Now all you need to do is type **sup** and press Enter (Return). You'll see the trademark symbol elevated as superscript text. In the same way, you can create subscript text (for example, H_2O). Instead of typing sup, this time you type **sub**. The selected text is wrapped with the <sup> or <sub> tag pairs, respectively.

    BACKTRACKING TO HTML

From the get-go, Dreamweaver MX 2004 seems firmly entrenched in the land of CSS. What's a poor designer to do when a client with a <font> tag–based site comes a knockin'? You can switch back to working with <font> tags by altering a preference. From the General category of Preferences, clear the Use CSS Instead of HTML tags check box. You don't even have to restart Dreamweaver—just click OK and you're back in the land of <font> tags. Aren't you the <b> explorer?

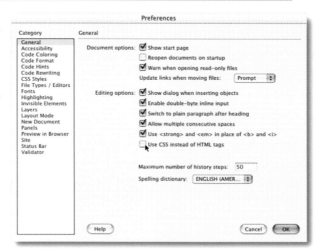

MY FAVORITE SNIPPET

Since Dreamweaver MX, users have
pleaded with Macromedia to add support for keyboard shortcuts for snippets. Macromedia has heard these pleas
and granted this feature request. Select
Edit > Keyboard Shortcuts and then
choose Snippets in the Commands
drop-down list. Click on the categories
to expand them, until you find the snippet you want. After you've located the
snippet, click on it. Now you just need
to assign the shortcut the same way
you normally would by pressing the key
combination you'd like to use. It may be
challenging finding a combo that isn't
already in use. I've found that

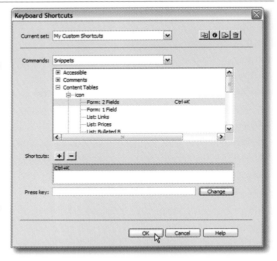

Ctrl+Shift+Alt (Command+Shift+Option) combined with almost any single character
usually works.

CLICK-N-DRAG OBJECTS

Some objects found in the Insert bar are available only in Design view. For this tip, most
objects will work in either Code or Design view; just be sure to give either view focus before
you try this. Did you know that you can click the objects in the Insert bar and then drag
them into position within the Code or Design view? This may not sound useful at first
because you could just position your cursor and click the object to insert it. If you're like me,
you click the button, and then realize, "Oops, that's not where I want to put this." Too late
now—you've got to Edit > Undo or Ctrl+Z (Command+Z) and try again. Instead of releasing
that click, you could drag the object where you want the object to be inserted. A note of
warning (wooooooooooo): Be sure not to drag an object onto a bunch of selected code. If
you do, the object is going to eat your code for lunch—one meal you'll want to avoid.

TAG CHOOSER

The Tag Chooser is the last icon in the Common category of the Insert bar. If you wanted to, you could actually build the entire structure of your document from this single object. Tags are categorized on the left of the Tag Chooser dialog box. If a folder is selected, all tags display on the right; if a subcategory is selected, a more specific list of tags appears there. All you have to do is choose a tag and click Insert.

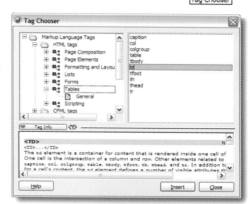

If there is a Tag Editor dialog available for the chosen tag, it displays next; otherwise, the Tag Chooser dialog box retains focus. You can keep adding tags to your heart's content—just be sure your cursor is positioned where you want the tag to be inserted. If you need to know more about the currently selected tag, click the Tag Info button to expand the dialog box to display reference material if available or use the Reference panel icon instead. When you're finished adding tags, click Close. It's just that easy.

PUTTING A DENT IN THE CODE, OR TAKING THEM OUT

Neatly formatted code is far easier to read and troubleshoot than messy code. Part of what makes code neat is the care that developers take when indenting lines. If Commands > Apply Source Formatting doesn't quite get it right, you do have the option to do additional formatting manually. I find these shortcuts most helpful when hand-coding JavaScript or server-side code. There is a better combo of keyboard shortcuts than the old Tab or Shift+Tab combo, which doesn't require any selection at all to indent or outdent entire lines of code. Try using Ctrl+Shift+> (Command+Shift+>) to indent the line(s) or Ctrl+Shift+< to outdent the line(s). To help you remember which shortcut is which, the angle is pointing to the direction the code will be moved.

   CHECK THIS OUT AT THE LIBRARY

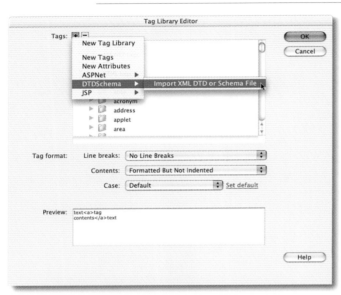

Although the Tag Library Editor is wonderful for tweaking your code, it really begins to shine in its capability to accept custom tags. Choose Edit > Tag Libraries to see all the current tags and make their settings available for modification. You could truly spend days here getting your code just the way you want it. To add a tag, select its language (or insert your own) and choose Add (+). After you define a tag, you can add attributes to it. Now, if you really want to see some power, how would you like to add a whole slate of tags and attributes at once? You can do exactly that if you have, at hand or online, a DTD or schema for the language. For example, I was able to add all the tags and attributes for SMIL (Synchronized Multimedia Integration Language) by down-loading the files from the W3C site. Total operation time: about 23 seconds.

   DO NOT PASS GO, GO DIRECTLY TO LINE NUMBER

We've all had pages that contain a JavaScript error at some point. When the browser tells us that we have an error on a specific line number, we're anxious to look at that line to see what is causing the trouble. Don't bother scrolling to get there, just use the Go to Line Number command, which is only enabled when Code view has focus. Select View > Go to Line Number or use the Ctrl+G (Command+G) key-

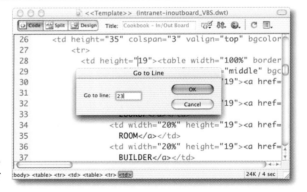

board shortcut. When the Go to Line Number dialog appears, type the line number and press Enter (Return) or click OK. The document scrolls (if necessary) and your cursor is placed at the start of the specified line number. The Go to Line Number command proves especially handy when you're working in long documents with hundreds of lines of code.

    D'LEFT AND D'RIGHT

When you need to delete some text or code you probably press and hold the Backspace
key or the Delete key depending on if you need to remove code from the left or the right of
the cursor's current position. Sometimes you may even hold the key down for what seems
like an eternity before you've removed all of the code. You can speed this process up significantly by holding down the Ctrl (Command) key while pressing Delete (to remove a word
to the right of the cursor) or Backspace (to remove a word to the left of the cursor). Try it;
you'll like it.

    WHERE'S THAT FUNCTION?

JavaScript files can get
mighty complicated and
lengthy. Keeping track of
where you put which func-
tion so that you can go back
to it easily requires an excellent memory—or
Dreamweaver's assistance.
Located in the Document
toolbar is the Code
Navigation icon (that's the
one that looks like a pair of
curly braces and is enabled
only while editing code).

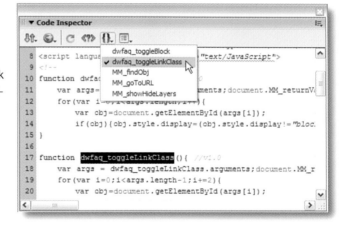

When clicked, the Code Navigation icon displays a drop-down list containing the names of
all the functions in the current document. The functions listed may be either JavaScript or
VBScript and are in the order in which they appear on the page. I've formed the habit of
using Ctrl+Click (Command+Click), which sorts all functions alphabetically, making it much
easier to find what I'm looking for. As you might expect, selecting a listed function takes you
right to it in the code—exceptionally convenient!

CHAPTER 9 • Maxing Out Your Code **199**

   PUT YOUR HEADS TOGETHER

It sure can feel like a boring chore to attach CSS files and add external JavaScript and `<meta>` tags to each new document you create for a site. You could go directly to the code and copy and paste what you need, but there is a simpler way that even works while you are in Design view. (Remember that you can hand-code in Design view, too.)

First select View > Head Content or press Ctrl+Shift+H (Command+Shift+H) to enable the Head Content bar if it is not already visible (in both documents you're working with). Each tag is represented by an icon. Click the icon of the tag you want to copy to the other document. Select Edit > Copy or press Ctrl+C (Command+C). Switch to the second document and click anywhere on the Head Content bar that is not occupied by another icon and then paste using either Edit > Paste or Ctrl+V (Command+V). Dreamweaver places the copied tag just before the closing `<head>` tag and its icon will appear last in the Head Content bar. Oh, you'd rather it appear where you want it in the first place? Okay, no problem—you can do that. Don't click an empty area of the Head Content; instead, click an existing icon and paste, and the copied code will be placed just before the selection you made.

   SWITCHING TAGS

Every now and then there comes a time when you need to change a tag to an entirely different tag. Let's say you have a `<p>` tag that you need to change to a `<div>` tag. Right-click (Ctrl+Click) the tag in the tag selector and choose Edit Tag. All you have to do is change the opening tag and give focus back to the document. You'll see that Dreamweaver has updated the code, changing the closing tag to match the value of the opening tag you typed.

   COMPLETE WITHOUT YOU

It has happened to me and I've seen it happen to others too. Sometimes Dreamweaver is just a tad too helpful when it comes to tag completion. Upon completing an opening tag I usually do want a closing tag. There are instances where I don't want the tag completion (perhaps because the end tag will come after some existing content), but it isn't worth disabling the feature in Preferences. When the end tag is added it is easy to forget that Ctrl+Z (Command+Z) will undo the tag completion that Dreamweaver has done for you. Just because Dreamweaver adds the end tag doesn't mean you can't undo it. After all, you're in control.

   BACK AND FORTH

This is probably the quickest way to get to exactly where you need to be in the code to do your editing and get back to Design view when done. Instead of scrolling through Code view to get where you need to be, first click in Design view and then press Ctrl+Backquote (Command+Backquote) to switch to the area of Code view that corresponds to the cursor's position in Design view. (Never heard of Backquote before? It's the same as the Tilde [~] key.) Use the same shortcut to jump to the place in Design view that corresponds to Code view. If you're the menu-using type, you could use View > Switch Views to toggle back and forth between Code and Design views. If you're using Code and Design views simultaneously (also known as Split view), your cursor position is all that changes, but if you're using one view or another, the actual view changes and places your cursor accordingly.

   DO YOU VALIDATE?

For the most part, Dreamweaver does an excellent job of keeping your code valid and properly written; however, Dreamweaver can only do so much itself. The rest is up to us to tell Dreamweaver what we want done or hand-code it ourselves. In the Validation panel, Dreamweaver can check your document against various validation specs and list warnings and errors for you. Select File > Check Page > Validate Markup or use the keyboard shortcut Shift+F6 to begin the process. A list of errors and warnings appears in the Validation panel, of which you can double-click to jump to that line number in the code—even if you're in Design view. If you're not sure what any of the listed items mean from their descriptions alone, select the entry and then use the Options menu or right-click (Ctrl+Click) to select More Info. In the same menu as More Info, you will find Settings, where you can pick and choose which types of validation checking should be done.

    NOTE TO SELF...

The Dreamweaver Design Notes feature is touted as a tool for communicating in a team of developers. But if you're flying solo or just feeling a little antisocial, you don't have to use it that way. Instead of making a backup copy of a file and cluttering a site with multiple versions of a file, create a Design Note instead. It is always a good idea to back up your site before making edits, but this quick-and-dirty method is suitable in many cases. One word of caution: If Design Notes are uploaded to the server, they are publicly (although not obviously) accessible; do not put any private info into a Design Note.

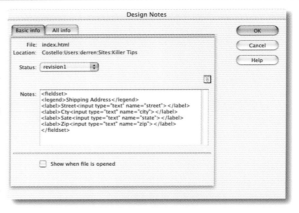

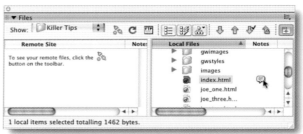

To add a Design Note, right-click (Ctrl+Click) the file in the Files panel and select Design Notes from the context menu or double-click in the Notes column to the right of the file with which you want the Design Note to be associated. Paste the code into the text area and check the box if you'd like the Design Note to appear each time the file is opened; click OK when you're done. Unless you've disabled Design Notes in your site definition, you should see an icon in the Notes column of the expanded Files panel.

Double-click that icon anytime you need to view the note. Now you know exactly where to look for information about that particular file. By the way, Design Notes work on all file types listed in your Files panel. Feel free to add any type of notation you need, be it reminders, file status, backup code, or anything else you can imagine. There is one cool thing you can do with a Design Note attached to a webpage that doesn't work with other file types: Click the Show When File Is Opened option on the Design Note dialog and your note pops up as a reminder whenever you (or anyone else) returns to work on the file.

  CREATE YOUR OWN CODE HINTS

If you're creating XML documents or making custom ColdFusion or ASP.Net tags, you'll find the custom code hints feature especially useful. Edit > Tag Libraries not only lets you add custom tags, attributes, and their values, it also gives you complete control over the format of your code. (See "Complete Formatting Control" on the next page in this chapter.)

Using the Tag Library Editor is rather straight-forward. Click the Add (+) button, select New Tags, and then choose the Tag Library folder you want to add a tag to from the drop-down list. Now type the tag name, check the box if it should have a closing tag, and then click OK. The tag is represented by a folder within the Tag Library you chose. If the new tag has potential attributes or you want to add attributes to an existing tag, click the Add (+) button again, and choose New Attributes. Now select the Tag Library and

the tag from the respective drop-down list, and then type the attribute and click OK. Did you notice that the menu says tags and attributes, both plural? Try entering multiple tags or attributes separated by a comma. You can add as many tags or attributes at one time as you like.

It gets even better; you can even add the type of values the attribute should suggest. Locate the tag in the tree menu and find the attribute you want to assign a type of value. After you've selected the attribute, you'll see an option to set the case of the attribute and a preview, but we're interested in the Attribute Type field. Most of your options should make sense to you, but I encourage you to make a fake tag with attributes of various types so that you know what to expect. The one that may not make sense right away is Enumerated. This is the only option that will enable the Values field, where you can type a comma-separated list of possible attribute values. These values appear in a drop-down list when you're hand-coding the value, just like the align attribute pops up a list of center, justify, left, or right.

COMPLETE FORMATTING CONTROL

Because you're now familiar with the Tag Library Editor from the "Create Your Own Code Hints" tip, I thought you might want to know just a little bit more about what you can do with it. The default source formatting can sometimes yield undesirable results. Before Dreamweaver MX, you had to manually edit a certain file to get any sort of custom formatting—with quite a bit of trial and error. Now all it takes is selecting the tag in the Tag Library Editor, and then selecting Line Breaks, Contents and Case settings. Just remember that a tag's formatting depends not only on its own settings but the setting of Contents for the parent element containing the tag. You even get to see an example of how the code will look in the Preview field.

CODE SURVEILLANCE

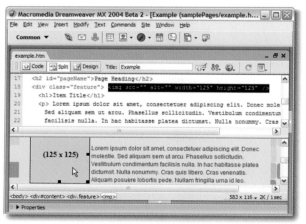

The sooner you start spying on your code, the better off you'll be. That's right, spy on it. Unless you have good reason, your code should always be visible to you while you're working. Why? Because I said so. Is that not a good enough answer? Oh okay, I'll tell you why…there's much more to good web development than what you see in Design view. Learning what powers your page, the code, will help you to become a much better developer. When it comes time to troubleshoot a problem, you'll know where to look. Even if you don't know any code at all to start, by watching Dreamweaver create the code for you, eventually the code will start making sense for you. Before you know it, you'll be getting your toes wet so to speak and eventually diving into the code to do your own customizations. Dreamweaver lets you choose between Code view, Design view, or Split view by clicking the respective buttons in the Document toolbar or by selecting the view of choice from one of the first three entries in the View menu.

   ## RECOVERING SNIPPETS FROM DREAMWEAVER MX

One of the favorite Dreamweaver features among hand-coders is the Snippets panel. When you installed Dreamweaver MX 2004, it probably wasn't long before you noticed that all your snippets from Dreamweaver MX weren't transferred. Not to worry, we'll get them all back for you in a jiffy.

Hopefully you kept your snippets in Dreamweaver MX organized. It is much easier if you have all your custom snippets in one folder. In Dreamweaver MX, add a new folder to your Snippets panel called MySnippets, and then drag all of your existing custom snippets to this folder. It's okay to drag folders filled with snippets to MySnippets.

Okay, now that you're organized, you need to locate your custom snippets on your hard drive. You'll find them in your user Dreamweaver MX configuration, under the Snippets folder. If you need extra help finding your Dreamweaver MX snippets, use your operating system's search to find a

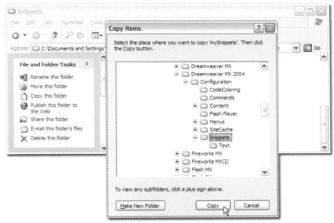

folder named MySnippets. Now just copy the MySnippets folder from your Dreamweaver MX user configuration and paste it to your Dreamweaver MX 2004 user configuration under the Snippets folder. If there isn't a Snippets folder, go ahead and create one manually first and then paste. If you thought this was a real bother, I suggest you do like I have and suggest that Macromedia add an import\export feature to the Snippets panel (wish-dreamweaver@macromedia.com).

Moving on
Down the Road

I never got into souping up or detailing cars when I was growing up—and, considering that my first car was a Pacer, that's probably a good thing. Perhaps that explains why I'm so crazy

Moving on Down the Road:

Integrating and Extending Dreamweaver

about the options in Dreamweaver for customization and extensibility. This stuff just (pick one)…(a) rocks my world, (b) floats my boat, or (c) christens my cabbage. (Sorry about that last one; I'm trying to start a new cliché and this one obviously needs some work.)

In this chapter, we've tried to collect for you the best tips from the realm that takes Dreamweaver to the next level. Consequently, you'll find tips for folks just starting out with customization by creating commands via the History panel (right next to the strategies for building floating panels). You'll also find some cool methods for customizing Dreamweaver that could actually make you some cash. Show you the money, you say? Just consider this chapter to be all over the map—and customizing and extending Dreamweaver takes a pretty big map—and use it as your guide to buried treasure.

Before you continue, read this quick note from our lawyers: Be forewarned that the investigation and usage of Macromedia Dreamweaver extensionology and customizabilitization is extremely addictive and could cause loss of sleep and momentary bouts of frustration coupled with vast stretches of oh-my-gosh-I-can't-believe-it-actually-works!-itis. Proceed at your own risk. Eat your vegetables. Christen the Cabbage.

  STRUCTURING HISTORY PANEL–CREATED COMMANDS

Don't you just hate to do the same task over and over again? I do, and that's why I'm a History panel fanatic. Not only does the History panel give a clear picture of almost every step you take in Dreamweaver, you also can easily transform those steps into a repeatable command. Years of building macros in Word taught me one basic rule to automating changes: End where you want to begin. Let's say you have a standard list of names that you want to put in lastname-comma-firstname order. All you need do in Dreamweaver is perform the operation on the first name—using only your keyboard, as the History panel doesn't record mouse clicks—and end by positioning the cursor so that it's ready to do the second line. In this case, here's what I would do:

1. Place the cursor in front of the first name.
2. Shift-select the first name.
3. Cut it.
4. Move to the end of the last name.
5. Type in a comma and a space.
6. Paste the first name.
7. Move your cursor in front of the **next** first name.

At this point, either select the steps in the History panel and click Replay or—if you see a continuing use for this operation—choose the Save Selected Steps as a Command option. Either way, you're good to go, again and again and again.

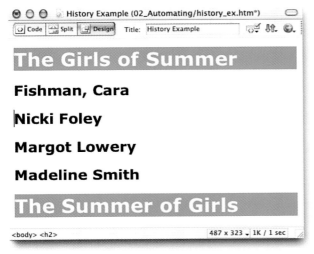

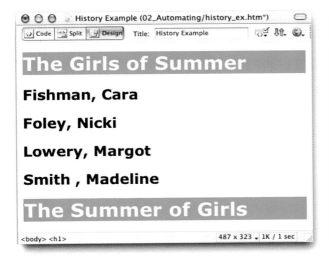

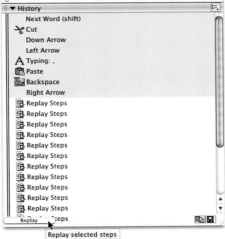

 SHOW MORE LAYERS

Sometimes you may find a dialog that you wish were just a little different. Take the Show-Hide Layers Behavior, for example. Most of the time I have more than four layers in a document when I need this behavior, and I always have to scroll to find the layer I need. Thankfully I'm not stuck with the dialog the way it is because the interface is nothing more than a simple HTML file that I can customize.

Before you customize any files that reside in Dreamweaver's main configuration folder, always make a backup. You may think the change is insignificant, but you never know what might go wrong. Now that I've got the usual disclaimer out of the way, let's open up Dreamweaver MX 2004\Configuration\Behaviors\Actions\Show-Hide Layers.htm in Dreamweaver. Usually I have more then four layers to work with and I don't like to scroll if it can be avoided. So, let's make the Named Layers field much taller. Select the field in Design view, and then in the List/Menu Property inspector, change the Height from 4 to 12 (or however many lines you'd like). When you're done, save the file and restart Dreamweaver to see your change in effect.

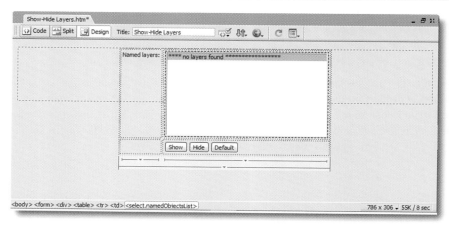

ALIAS: THE DREAMWEAVER COMMAND

Look out XHTML, there's a new sheriff in town and you'd better clean up your act. An old Dreamweaver workhorse command, Clean Up HTML, has been enhanced to also handle XHTML pages. Found under the Commands menu, this handy feature obligingly changes its name according to the page

type: When a regular HTML page is the current one, you'll see Clean Up HTML in the menu; XHTML page users will see Clean Up XHTML. No matter what it's called, this command is great to run first when you get a page handed off to you and then again in the final stages of page design. With Clean Up HTML/XHTML, you can rid your page of unused tag pairs (such as `<h2>...</h2>`) and redundant nested tags. The command also can strip out HTML comments whether they are the standard variety or Dreamweaver-specific comments. Be careful if you decide to go the latter route, however; removing Dreamweaver-inserted comments will also remove any template or Library item functionality. One last tip for the Clean Up HTML/XHTML command: If you want to remove specific tags, just enter the text of the tag and not the full tag (for example, enter **b** for the bold tag rather than **<b>**). For multiple tags, enter them in a space-separated list, such as **b i u**.

  ## AN OBJECT LOVE AFFAIR

An extension developer never forgets his or her first time. My first was twins—a matched set of objects to replace the `<sup>` and `<sub>` tags missing from Dreamweaver. I was really enamored of objects during that time and picked up some pointers I'm more than willing to pass on to you. First, let me just recommend that for any tag or code that does not require a user interface, you use snippets rather than objects. What, has he completely spurned his first love? No, it's just that objects require a bit of coding, and snippets are, as we used to say down south, dirt simple. When you do begin to build your objects, remember that you have to place all objects in a folder within the Dreamweaver MX 2004\Configuration\Objects folder; you can use one of the existing folders or create your own. Moreover, the folder structure can go only one level deep. Unlike with custom behaviors, you can't create submenu items by nesting folders. Finally, if you're really interested in working with objects, take apart a number of the objects included in Dreamweaver. There are many excellent examples of everything from the most basic to exceedingly advanced objects.

    CUSTOM EMPTY TAGS

It is no big secret that you can add custom tags to Dreamweaver using the Tag Library Editor (see "Create Your Own Code Hints" in Chapter 9). If you need to create an "empty tag"—that is, a tag that doesn't have an end tag that requires closing, such as `<br />`—the Tag Library Editor does not give you an option to ensure the forward slash is used. It is a very little known secret that the underlying support for empty tags is already in place despite the lack of interface for it. Go ahead and take advantage of the Tag Library Editor to add all of your tags first. Then go and dig up the .vtm file for each new tag requiring modification in your user's configuration. Let's say you created a `<love>` tag. In love.vtm, you'll find something like this:

```
<tag name="love" endtag="yes" tagtype="nonempty">
<tagformat nlbeforetag="0" nlaftertag="0" />
<attributes></attributes>
</tag>
```

In order for it to output `<love />` instead of `<love>`, you'll need to modify the first line to read:

```
<tag name="love" endtag="xml" tagtype="empty">
```

After you restart Dreamweaver, give the new tag a trial run by right-clicking (Ctrl+Clicking) in code view and choosing Insert Tag. Find your tag in the Tag Chooser dialog and select it; then click the Insert button. You'll see that the tag is properly closed and your cursor is positioned just before the forward slash so that you can add any required attributes if applicable. You'll have to remember to manually close the tag in Code view, though, or Dreamweaver will try to add an ending tag.

     ## A PLUS IN YOUR COLUMN

Websites being developed by teams have special challenges, such as being able to quickly see which pages are already done and which still need work. Dreamweaver's Files panel has customizable columns that can help keep everyone on the team clued in. To add a custom column, start in the Files panel in Expanded mode. Windows users should then choose View > File View Columns, and Mac users should select Site > Site Files View > File View Columns from the main menu. After you have the File View Columns category of the Site Definitions dialog box on the screen, choose Add (+) to insert a custom column. Give your new column a name in the Column Name field and add a design note in the Associate with Design Note field. Change the alignment if you don't want to use the default Left position and make sure that the Show option is selected. When you return to the Files panel, you'll see that your new column is added for all files. To enter a column value for a file, click twice slowly in the column—a regular double-click opens the file. For a column showing the page's completion status, I prefer to use decimal numbers rather than words; I find that .10, .50, and .75 are properly sorted and more accurately tell the status rather than "almost done" or "nearly finished." So, with this system, how is a completed page labeled? Why, any developers worth their salt know that when it's done, it's 1.0.

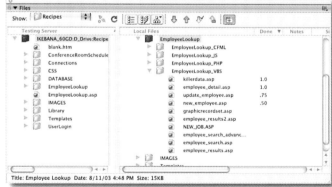

   THE MOTHER OF ALL MENUS

All of the menus found in Dreamweaver—including the main menu, all the panel menus, and the context menus—are controlled by a single XML file. Found in the Dreamweaver MX 2004\Configuration\Menus folder, the menus.xml file is truly a mother lode of information and power. Want to know how Dreamweaver really executes a command? Check out the command's menu entry in menus.xml to see the file used or actual code executed. You can open and examine the file in Dreamweaver. But—paste enormous warning sticker here—if you plan on modifying it, be sure to open the version found in the Dreamweaver MX 2004 user's folder. You should also be sure to make a backup just in case of trouble; and if you really get in trouble, there is a Macromedia-created backup in the same folder called menus.bak that will get you back on the right footing. After you've opened the file, you'll notice that all the shortcut definitions are at the top of the file. In my experience, these are best modified using the Keyboard Shortcut Editor found under the Edit menu. The fastest way I've found to get to the main menu definitions is to search for "Main Window" (with or without the quotation marks) using the Dreamweaver Find and Replace feature. Happy menu spelunking!

```
menus.xml                                                           _  ⯐ ✕
  ⟨⟩ Code   Split   Design   🐾   Title:                  ᘓ ⩔ 🌐   C ▣
1794
1795  <menubar name="Main Window" id="DWMainWindow">
1796      <menu name="Apple" id="DWMenu_Apple" platform="mac">
1797          <menuitem name="About Macromedia Dreamweaver MX 2004" command="dw.showAboutBox()" enabled="true"
1798      </menu>
1799      <menu name="_File" id="DWMenu_File">
1800          <menuitem name="_New..." key="Cmd+N" domRequired="false" enabled="true" command="dw.newDocument(
1801          <menuitem name="_Open..." key="Cmd+O" domRequired="false" enabled="dw.getDocumentDOM() == null |
1802          <menu name="Open Recen_t" id="DWMenu_File_RecentFiles">
1803            <menuitem dynamic name="(No Recent Files)" file="Menus/MM/File_RecentFiles.htm" id="DWMenu_Fil
1804          </menu>
1805          <menuitem name="Open in _Frame..." key="Cmd+Shift+O" enabled="dw.canOpenInFrame()" command="dw.o
1806          <menuitem name="_Close" key="Cmd+W" enabled="dw.getDocumentDOM() != null" command="dw.closeDocum
1807          <menuitem name="_Close" key="Cmd+W" enabled="dw.getFocus() != 'none'" command="if (dw.getFocus()
1808          <menuitem name="Clos_e All" enabled="dw.getDocumentDOM() != null" command="dw.closeAll()" id="DW
1809          <separator />
1810          <menuitem name="_Save" key="Cmd+S" file="Menus/MM/File_Save.htm" id="DWMenu_File_Save" />
1811          <menuitem name="Save _As..." key="Cmd+Shift+S" file="Menus/MM/File_SaveAs.htm" id="DWMenu_File_S
1812          <menuitem name="Save to Rem_ote Server..." enabled="dw.getDocumentDOM() != null" command="dw.sav
1813          <menuitem name="Save as Template..." file="Menus/MM/File_SaveAsTemplate.htm" id="DWMenu_File_Sav
1814          <menuitem name="Save A_ll" enabled="dw.canSaveAll()" command="dw.saveAll()" id="DWMenu_File_Save
◀                     ⠿                                                ▶
<menubar>                                                          1K / 1 sec
```

     ## WHAT ELSE IS ON THE MENU?

If you decide to explore the depths of the Dreamweaver menu structure, you should know a few things first about the format of the controlling file, menus.xml. First, every main item (there are 10 in the standard Dreamweaver menu: File, Edit, View, and so on) contains a list of separate menu items. Each menu item contains a unique `id` attribute and an optional keyboard shortcut. Whether the menu item is displayed is controlled by the `enabled` attribute; if the `enabled` attribute evaluates as true, the item is available; if it's false, the menu item is disabled. What determines the function of a menu item? There are two possible, mutually exclusive attributes: `command` and `file`. The `command` attribute takes a JavaScript function, often a Dreamweaver API call; for example, the `command` value for the File > Save All menu item is `dw.saveAll()`. The second attribute, `file`, points to a HTML file in the Dreamweaver MX 2004\Configuration folder—either the main or the user's configuration—which contains JavaScript too complex to fit in a single line or opens a dialog box. When you are modifying the menus.xml file, take extreme care to properly code your entries (not to mention always work with a backup at the ready). Dreamweaver disables the menu items containing any entries with incorrect syntax. For complete details, see Help > Extensions> Extending Dreamweaver.

   THIRD-PARTY TAG, YOU'RE IT!

Look up any good reference of HTML and you're going to get a standard set of tags. But, because HTML is so flexible—and browsers are so tolerant of tags they don't understand—extension developers often employ a healthy dose of non-HTML or third-party tags. When might a third-party tag be used? Here's one example: I co-developed a Dreamweaver extension called Deva, which builds navigation systems, such as table of contents and indexes. With Deva, any text can be marked as an index item, which surrounds the text with a `<index>`...`</index>` tag pair. The `<index>` tag is a Deva third-party tag and, as such, highlights the enclosed text. The highlight enables the designer to quickly identify specially marked passages. Third-party tags are defined by enclosing an XML file in the Dreamweaver MX 2004\Configuration\ThirdPartyTags folder. Here's the entry for the Deva `<index>` tag:

```
<tagspec tag_name="index" tag_type="nonempty"
  render_contents="true"
content_model="marker_model"></tagspec>
```

As an alternative to the highlighting option, third-party tags can also be represented by icons—in which case the `render_contents` attribute would be `false` and a .gif image, also stored in the ThirdPartyTags folder, is specified.

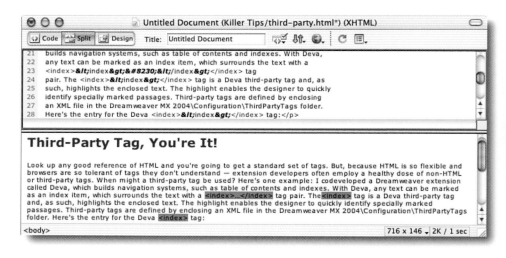

     FREE SCRIPTS, GET YOUR FREE SCRIPTS RIGHT HERE!

Pssssttt! Want a great collection of JavaScript functions and utilities guaranteed to ramp up your extensibility productivity? I can let you have it for a song…and that song is "Dreamweaver," of course. Included with every installation of Dreamweaver are a terrific number of JavaScript files containing a key functionality for almost every operation an extension developer needs. Why is it so extensive? Simple—because these scripts are the same ones used by the Macromedia engineers to give Dreamweaver its power. You'll find the scripts in the Dreamweaver MX 2004\Configuration\Shared folder in a couple of places. The older but still useful scripts are found in the Shared\MM\Scripts folder; the newer ones are in the Shared\Common\Scripts folder. There are too many scripts and functions to describe here, but one of my favorites is enableControl.js, found in the Shared\MM\Scripts\ CMN folder. In Dreamweaver, this function is used by the Master Detail Page Set application object, among others. After you include this file, you're programmatically able to enable or disable a dialog's form controls by calling a single function. It's the essence of schweet.

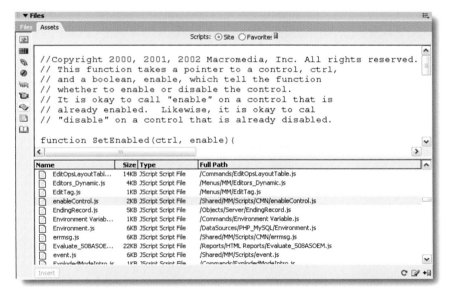

   REPLACING WITHIN RESULTS

Sooner or later, you'll do a Find and Replace (Edit > Find and Replace), but your search will yield far more results than what needs changing. Most everyone I've asked will open each file and carefully execute each replace. Everyone else uses fancy regular expressions to get exactly what they're after, which can take longer than what you are about to learn how to do.

Suppose you have too many results from a search you've performed. Bring back the Find and Replace dialog by clicking the green arrow on the left of the Results panel. In the list of search results in the Results panel, Ctrl+Click (Command+Click) individual noncontiguous results, or Shift+Click once and then a second time to select all results between and including the ones you Shift+Clicked. Now choose Replace (I said Replace, not Replace All) in the Find and Replace dialog. The files that are modified get marked by a green dot to the left of the filenames in the Results panel. Just think of all the time you'll save from this tip alone!

As with any Find and Replace you perform in files that aren't open, make sure you make a backup first, just in case.

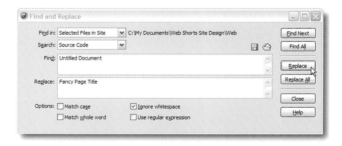

   COLOR ME EXTENSIBLE

If you've looked at all into creating your own Dreamweaver extensions, you may be aware that the user interface for them is based on HTML forms. This counts as an entry in both the plus and the minus columns; it's an advantage because that makes it easy to build interfaces right in Dreamweaver, and it's a disadvantage because HTML form elements are pretty limited in functionality. The Dreamweaver engineers have heard the cries of woe of extension authors everywhere and responded with some nifty additional controls. Top of my list is the color picker. The color picker is used throughout the Dreamweaver interface. Whenever the user needs to choose a color, that little box pops open a whole palette of colors, complete with an eye-dropper for sampling. You can add a color picker to your extension by dropping code like this in your HTML form:

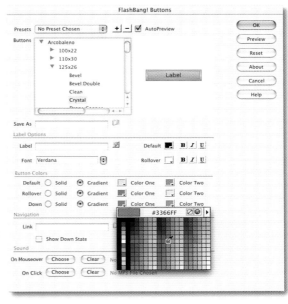

```
<input type="mmcolorbutton" name="myColorPicker" value="">
```

You need to specify an `<input>` tag with a type attribute of `mmcolorbutton` and a unique name. The `value` attribute is optional; without it, the user sees the default gray color. You are, of course, free to specify a value to preset the color, if you like. Make mine puce, please.

   EDITABLE AND SELECTABLE? INCREDIBLE!

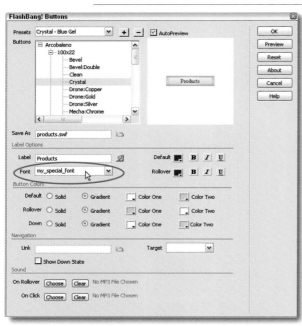

Looking for a cool input control? I know, it's what you live for. Well, here's one that I've long lusted for. Many of the drop-down lists used on standard program user interfaces (not web applications) allow users to type in their own value if they don't see something they like in the list. In the trade, this is known as an editable select list. To convert a `<select>` list in Dreamweaver to editable format takes years of training and several man-years of labor. Or, you could just add these attributes to the tag: `editable="true" edit-text="some default value"`. You must use the `edittext` attribute, but you can leave the value empty. That's it. Now all the items on the list are editable. Often, a user interface design might call for the first item in the list to be blank, indicating that it's editable. In such cases, the `<select>` tag would look like this:

```
<select name="mainList" editable="true"
edittext="">
```

As with standard `<select>` lists, the `selectedIndex` property is used to determine which item the user chose. If an editable list item was selected, the `selectedIndex` is equal to –1. The following statement says, "If the selected index is –1, we know that the text was input by the user. Otherwise, they must have chosen something that was already in the list."

```
var theSelect = dwscripts.findDOMObject("theSelectName");
var retVal;
if(theSelect.selectedIndex == -1){
retVal = theSelect.editText;
}
else{
retVal = theSelect.options[ theSelect.selectedIndex] .value;
}
```

If you're unfamiliar with the `dwscripts.FindDOMObject` code used above, see "Finding Objects" also in this chapter.

  ## MYSTERY OF THE MXP

You know that extension files are delivered in the MXP file format for installation via the Extension Manager, but how do you make an MXP? After you have your extension created, you only need one more file to create an extension package. A special XML file, the MXI file, is required to make an extension complete. The MXI file holds all the data required by the Extension Manager, as well as instructions where to put the files in

Dreamweaver's Configuration folder. Help in creating your MXI file is not far away; choose Help > Extensions > Creating and Submitting Extensions to find out all you need to know about creating and submitting extensions to the Macromedia Exchange. For help with the MXI file format, look at Step 4 in the Creating and Submitting Extensions help file, where you'll find a link to the MXI file format PDF.

   ## VALID MXI

The Extension Manager won't package your extension unless your MXI file is well-formed XML. Internet Explorer can help you find where you've made an error when the extension won't package. Temporarily rename the .mxi file with an .xml extension, and then preview it in Internet Explorer. Error messages usually give you some indication of what you need to fix. Typical errors include invalid nested tags, uppercase tag names or attributes, and unclosed quotation marks. Keep refreshing the page as you fix the file until you no longer see an error message and your file is well-formed XML.

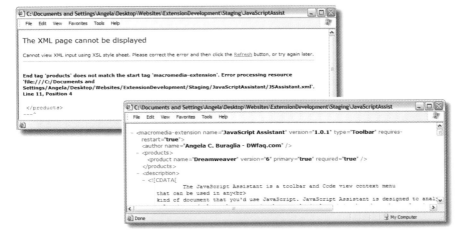

   RETURN OF THE CODE NAVIGATOR

If you're a Tolkien fan, *Return of the King* is the crowning (no pun intended, really!) achievement. For hardcore coders, Return of the Code Navigator resonates just as deeply. The Code Navigator was a function found on the Document toolbar that listed all the functions in the current page; choose any function name to jump to its location in the code. Very powerful functionality with a fairly limited audience. In an effort to streamline the user interface, the Code Navigator was removed. Fret not, my guitar-loving friend (now that pun was intentional), you can restore this useful tool in a nonce.

To restore the Code Navigator, open the toolbars.xml file that lives in the Dreamweaver MX 2004\Configuration\Toolbars folder (that's the system folder, not the user one) in your handy-dandy text editor. Search for the phrase DW_CodeNav (make sure you search in Source Code, not Text)—that's the ID for the Code Navigator menu button. Notice that the `<menubutton>` entry has been commented out, thus removing it from view. To restore the functionality, either remove the comment code entirely—which also restores the Reference icon—or move the closing tag of the comment above the Code Navigator `<menubutton>` entry. Restart Dreamweaver and all hail the Code Navigator.

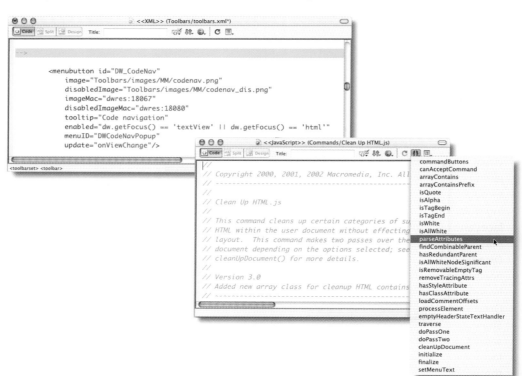

   ## HOT KEYS

By now you've probably discovered that you can edit all the Menu commands to your heart's content, but did you realize that you can customize other kinds of keyboard short-cuts too? Choose Edit > Keyboard Shortcuts and look at all the different options under the Commands drop-down list. Under the Code Editing option, you'll see a bunch of unassigned shortcuts for scrolling and making selections in Code view. I'm just wondering why I didn't discover these sooner! Go on, customize 'em, you know you want to.

   ## WHERE DOES HE GET THOSE FABULOUS TOYS?

A good 90% of creating a user interface for a Dreamweaver extension is made up of form elements: text fields, drop-down lists, radio buttons, and check boxes, among a few others. Interspersed in the interfaces are occasional graphics, such as the folder icon typically used to open the Select File dialog box. Unless you're building a completely different interface and avoiding all visual references to the Dreamweaver standard, it's less jarring to the user to retain the visual clues that are seen throughout the program. So should you go around tak-ing snapshots of the standard Dreamweaver user inter-faces and cut 'em up in a graphics program? Put down that cropping tool immediately! The kind folks from Dreamweaverland have done the work for you; you just need to know where to look. Most of the standard

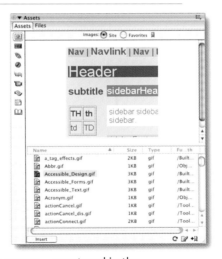

images—the folder icon, lightning bolt, and up and down arrows—are stored in the Dreamweaver MX 2004\Configuration\Shared folder in one of two folders: Shared\MM\Images or Shared\UltraDev\Images. Still can't find the image you know you've seen? Create a new site and point to the Dreamweaver MX 2004\Configuration folder as the local site root. Then, check the Images category of the Assets panel. All the graphics used throughout Dreamweaver (even some hidden Easter eggs) are there.

  TO RELOAD OR TO RESTART, THAT IS THE QUESTION…

Whether it is easier to reload than to suffer through a restart…I'll let you be the judge. This tip comes in handy both when you are developing extensions and want to test changes or after you install an extension. Don't expect it to work 100% of the time, but it does the job for most objects and commands—at least most of the time. The Reload Extensions option appears only if you Ctrl+Click (Option+Click) the Insert bar's category menu. Use the Reload Extensions trick whenever you install an object and the Extension Manager tells you that you have to restart Dreamweaver. If the object appears, great; but if it doesn't, you'll have to restart.

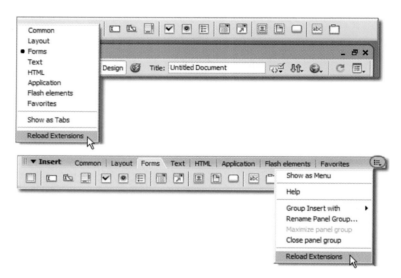

   ## FRESH RIPE COMMANDS READY FOR PICKIN'

I was first introduced to this trick by one of the best extension developers around, Massimo Foti. When developing commands, you'll be doing a lot of testing along the way and you will need to save often. Unless you refresh the Commands menu, the changes since the previous save will not be visible when you go to test the command. There is an easy way to refresh the commands list without having to restart Dreamweaver or wait for extensions to reload (covered in the previous tip). Select Commands > Edit Command List and when the dialog appears, just click the Close button. Now the command is fresh and ready for you to pick so that you can get a taste of whether it works the way you expect.

    I'M SORRY, IT'S NOT MY DEFAULT

The default extension for HTML documents in Dreamweaver MX 2004 is now .htm for both Windows and Macintosh. Although some may read this as another payment due He-Who-Lives-In-Seattle-And-Must-Not-Be-Named, others will just see it

as something they have to change so that they can continue to work as they used to. The default extension is listed on the New Document category of Preferences. The relevant link to the document type XML file provides some information in Dreamweaver Help, but isn't exactly crystal clear. (The previous sentence was lifted verbatim from the dictionary definition of "understatement.") So, here's the four-one-one: Open MMDocumentTypes.xml from the Dreamweaver MX 2004/Configuration/DocumentTypes folder; the XML file will open just fine in Dreamweaver itself. Look for the line that starts `<documenttype id="HTML"`…, and then locate the attribute for your OS (`winfileextension` or `macfileextension`). Make whatever file extension you want to be the default the first in the value list. If I want .html to be the default extension for Windows HTML docs, for example, the documenttype entry would read as follows:

```
<documenttype id="HTML" internaltype="HTML"
winfileextension="html,htm,shtml,shtm,stm,lasso,xhtml"
macfileextension="htm,html,shtml,shtm,lasso,xhtml" file="Default.html"
writebyteordermark="false">
```

I bolded the parts I changed to help you along. Don't say I didn't ever do anything for you now.

   TOO MANY ITEMS ON THE MENU TO CHOOSE

Whenever I go to a restaurant that offers too many items on the menu, I have a difficult time finding what I want. I feel the same way when I've got too many items listed in my Insert menu. Nearly all the objects in the Insert bar can be found in the Insert menu; and by the time you add more objects via extensions or your own creations, the list can get so long that it actually scrolls. You can shorten the list by removing the items you don't want. To do this, look through the Dreamweaver MX 2004\Configuration\Objects subfolders to find the .htm file for the object you don't want showing in the menu any more. Then open the file in Dreamweaver and add this code as the first line in the file:

```
<!-- MENU-LOCATION=NONE -->
```

Save the document and then restart Dreamweaver, or use the "To Reload or to Restart, That Is the Question" tip found earlier in this chapter. You can do the same thing for the Commands menu as well if you'd like. Just locate the file in Dreamweaver MX 2004\ Configuration\Commands. Now you can keep your menus neat and tidy, just the way you want them.

```
1 <!-- MENU-LOCATION=NONE -->
2 <html>
3 <head>
4 <!-- Copyright 2001 Macromedia, Inc. All rights reserved. -->
5 <title>Named Anchor</title>
```

   MULTIUSERS EQUALS MULTIPLE FILES

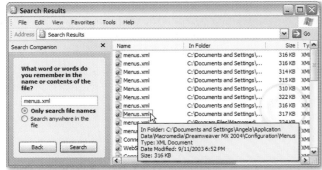

The support for multiuser configurations is great, but it can be a nightmare for extension developers as they are writing and testing their extensions. Dreamweaver checks the user's Configuration folder first for files and then looks in its own Configuration folder.* The user's files take precedence over those in the main Dreamweaver MX 2004 Configuration folder. First, I advise setting up your operating system to always show hidden files. (Check your operating system's help files for more information about showing hidden files and using its search interface.) Second, I suggest that you use your operating system's Search to find configuration files (such as menus.xml). If the results show that there is a file in the user's configuration and one in the Dreamweaver MX 2004 configuration, you'll know that you may need to edit one or both files.

I've given you the most important highlights and tips to find the right files. Although I wish I could give you more specifics, there is too much to say that won't all fit on this page. I recommend reading more about this in Help> Extensions> Extending Dreamweaver. Search for the word "multiuser" and read the section titled "About customizing Dreamweaver in a multiuser environment."

*Disclaimer: I've found only one instance where the program configuration overrides the user's configuration, but there may be others.

   BEHIND THE SCENES OF THE HISTORY PANEL

Many times when I'm working on an extension, I know there is an API call that does what I need, but I don't remember off the top of my head what it is. Digging through the extensibility documentation is one way to find out, but I've found that if I go behind the scenes of the History panel, I often can find what I am looking for. Let me show you what I mean. Open any document and make a few changes to it in Design view so that there are several steps listed in the History panel. Now go ahead and Ctrl+Shift+Click (Command+Shift+Click) anywhere inside the History panel. Did you see that? Do it a few times, it's fun. You'll see the JavaScript that Dreamweaver used to execute each step. Right-click (Ctrl+Click) a step and select Copy Steps from the context menu. If you try to paste in any open file in Dreamweaver, it will likely just execute the step as though you'd pressed the Replay button. Instead, paste to a plain-text file outside of Dreamweaver to view the code. This is a really great way to learn about Dreamweaver Extension API and see how Dreamweaver does its thing.

   FINDING OBJECTS

Whenever you write an extension that requires input from the user, you've got to have a form with at least one field. To get the value of the field, you first need to be able to find it. The old-fashioned way is to use `document.theFormName.theFieldName.value`.

If you add a link to the dwscripts.js file (located in Dreamweaver MX 2004\Configuration\Shared\Common\Scripts\), you can take advantage of Macromedia's `dwscripts.findDOMObject()` function. A link to the JavaScript file would look similar to the following code:

```
<script language=" src="../../Shared/MM/Scripts/dwsscripts.js"></script>
```

Now let's say you have a text field named theUsername. Instead of using the line `var myUsername = document.theForm.theUsername.value`, you would use `var myUsername = dwscripts.findDOMObject("theUsername").value`. This will give you support for the previous edition of Dreamweaver and the current version, which is all the Extension Manager supports anyhow.

  MAKING YOUR OWN NEW FROM TEMPLATE COMMAND

As promised in the tip "Whatever Happened to New From Template" here's how you'll be able to make your very own New from Template command:

1. Follow the tip "Multiusers Equals Multiple Files" earlier in this chapter to locate the menus.xml file. Back up and store the file in a safe place in case you need it later.

2. Open the original menus.xml file in Dreamweaver. Then Use Find to locate DWMenu_File, which should bring you close to line number 1728. This is the code from which the File menu is created.

3. Below the first `<menuitem>` tag, type the following tag:

```
<menuitem
name="New from Template..."
enabled= "true"
command="dw.newFromTemplate();"
domrequired="false"
id="YOURNAME_File_New_From_Template"
/>
```

Be sure to change YOURNAME to your own name or some other unique identifier. As a special touch, you could add a `<separator />` after the `<menuitem />` tag you added to make a horizontal rule below the menu item.

4. Save the document.

5. Restart Dreamweaver. Now when you look under the File menu, you should see New from Template as an option. Pretty simple, isn't it?

     TIME OUT FOR FLOATERS

Floaters. Sounds like jargon that might show up in a bad detective novel. Floaters, in the hard-boiled Dreamweaver world, are another type of extension. Now known as panels, floaters are so called because originally they floated above the interface and, unlike commands, stayed open and available while the page was being modified; Neil Clark's Flash Expressions panel, available from the Dreamweaver

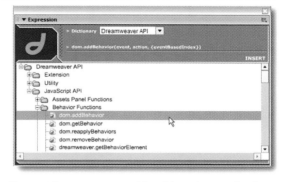

Exchange, is a good example of a custom floater. Floaters are capable of keeping track of selections and edits to the page via two built-in functions, selectionChanged() and documentEdited(); however, as you might imagine, both are processor-intensive activities and they need to be implemented with care. It's best to include a setTimeout() function to slightly delay processing so that Dreamweaver doesn't freeze up. (Check out Help > Extensions > Extending Dreamweaver for more info on the setTimeout() function and floaters.) One other aspect to watch out for when developing custom floaters: Be careful not to use a reserved name. Here's a list of names to avoid:

answers, assets, behaviors, btc, css_styles, data bindings, databases, debug, frames, ftplog, history, html, html_styles, layers, linkchecker, objects, properties, reference, reports, search, server_behaviors, server_components, site_files, sitespring, snippets, tag_inspector, tc, timelines, and *validation.*

   MY DOCUMENTS

Customizing documents to include things common to all pages you develop—such as copyright notices and `doctype`—ensures that you never forget to include the information and saves you all the time it would have taken to add the code for each new page. There are a bunch of document file types to choose from in New Document dialog, and they each have their very own default document in the configuration that can be customized to suit your needs. You can add whatever you want to the appropriate default file located in the Dreamweaver MX 2004\Configuration\DocumentTypes\NewDocuments folder. After you edit the file, save it and open a new file of its kind in Dreamweaver to verify that all your changes are what you expect.

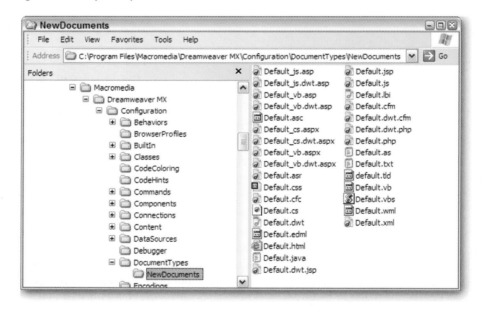

   ## ADDING CUSTOM TAGS TO THE TAG CHOOSER

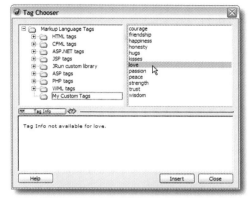

When registering custom tags you've created—be they XML, ColdFusion, .Net, or another language—the Tag Library Editor enables you to use the Attributes tab of the Tag inspector and code hints, but it can also offer you another feature if you know this trick…and you soon will! If you want to take advantage of the tag chooser with your custom tag, you need to do things a little differently when adding tags through Edit > Tag Libraries. Instead of adding to an existing tag library, you need to create your own tag library and store your custom tags there.

To start your own tag library, click the (+) button, and then choose New Tag Library. Give the tag library a name such as My Custom Tags or something more relevant, and then click OK. Now check the boxes for the document types you want to make your custom tags available in the Used In section. All ColdFusion custom tags must start with cf_, and ASP.Net custom tags always start with asp:. Some other server languages require a specific prefix for custom tags as well. You can save yourself some typing when adding tags by adding the prefix in the Tag Prefix field if one applies to your custom tags; if you've added a prefix, you won't have to enter it when adding new custom tags. You can now add tags and attributes as you normally would. (See the "Create Your Own Code Hints" tip in Chapter 9 for more information.)

Now that you've added your custom tags, you'll find them in the tag chooser listed in their tag library. If for some reason you just don't want to make your own tag library and would rather your custom tags appear in an existing tag library, you must create a TagChooser.xml file to do so. (That's also the starting point for creating your own Tag Editor dialogs for the chosen tags.) Choose Help > Extensions> Extending Dreamweaver, click the Index tab, enter **Tag Chooser**, and then click Display. You can then see what it takes to create a TagChooser.xml file and decide whether it is worth the trouble or whether you can just have your own tag library.

   ## RATED X: MACROMEDIA CODE EXPOSED

This tip is rated X for eXtremely sophisticated. If you feel the urge to change an existing Macromedia server behavior, you'll either need to make copies of all involved files and hand-code the changes, or try to do it through the Server Behavior Builder.

To get the server behavior to appear in the New Server Behavior dialog box, you must first modify its .edml file. Find the original server behavior's .edml file in the appropriate server model folder under Dreamweaver MX 2004\Configuration\ServerBehaviors\. You're looking for the .edml file that contains `hideFromBuilder="true"`. Change the `true` to `false`, save the file, and then restart Dreamweaver. Now click the Server Behavior panel's Add (+) button and then select New Server Behavior from the drop-down list. Yes, I noticed there was an Edit Server Behavior option. Don't use it on Macromedia's server behaviors! It is safer to copy an existing server behavior and just have your own version of it than to risk ruining the original server behavior.

  ## TOOLBAR WORDS, BE GONE!

Guess I'm just getting old and set in my ways, but I don't really need for the three different view icons (Code, Split, and Design) to be labeled. Like pretty much everything else in Dreamweaver, you can change it, if you just know where to look. The magic file in question is toolbars.xml, found in the Dreamweaver MX 2004/Configuration/Toolbar folder. Because you are monkeying around with a needed program file, make a backup of the file to avoid any potential disasters. When you have the file open, look for the first three `<radiobutton>` entries with the IDs of `DW_CodeView`, `DW_SplitView`, and `DW_DesignView`. In each one, remove the value from the `label` attribute so that the line reads as follows: `label = " "`

Save the toolbars.xml file and restart Dreamweaver. When the program relaunches, your Document toolbar will be free of any unwanted verbiage.

    ## RUNNING A COMMAND FROM AN OBJECT

You've made a History command or maybe even a command of your very own, but wouldn't it be nice if it could have its own little icon on the Insert bar? All you need to know is the filename of the command file in the Commands folder and you can make an object that calls a command.

1. Open the Insertbar.xml file found in your user configuration Objects folder. (See the "Multiusers Equals Multiple Files" tip earlier in this chapter for more details.)

2. Locate the category where you want the new object to appear.

3. Add this code and be sure to change each attribute's placeholder value appropriately:

```
<button
command="dw.runCommand('My Command File Name Here.htm',null);"
enabled=""
id="SomethingTotallyUnique"
image="theCategory\MyImageName.gif"
name="This Is The Tool Tip Text For The Object" />
```

An example of a button that calls the Add/Remove Netscape Resize fix is as follows:

```
<button
command="dw.runCommand('Add Remove NS Resize Fix.htm',null);"
enabled=""
id="killerTips_Add_Remove_NS_Resize_Fix"
image="Common\resizeFix.gif"
name="Add\Remove NS Resize Fix" />
```

A unique ID is required, and you need an 18×18-pixel image stored in the location specified by the `image` attribute.

4. Save the Insertbar.xml file, and then restart Dreamweaver.

VOICES THAT MATTER

VISIT OUR WEB SITE

WWW.NEWRIDERS.COM

On our Web site you'll find information about our other books, authors, tables of contents, indexes, and book errata. You will also find information about book registration and how to purchase our books.

EMAIL US

Contact us at this address: **nrfeedback@newriders.com**

- If you have comments or questions about this book
- To report errors that you have found in this book
- If you have a book proposal to submit or are interested in writing for New Riders
- If you would like to have an author kit sent to you
- If you are an expert in a computer topic or technology and are interested in being a technical editor who reviews manuscripts for technical accuracy

- To find a distributor in your area, please contact our international department at this address: **nrmedia@newriders.com**

- For instructors from educational institutions who want to preview New Riders books for classroom use. Email should include your name, title, school, department, address, phone number, office days/hours, text in use, and enrollment, along with your request for desk/examination copies and/or additional information.
- For members of the media who are interested in reviewing copies of New Riders books. Send your name, mailing address, and email address, along with the name of the publication or Web site you work for.

BULK PURCHASES/CORPORATE SALES

The publisher offers discounts on this book when ordered in quantity for bulk purchases and special sales. For sales within the U.S., please contact: Corporate and Government Sales (800) 382-3419 or **corpsales@pearsontechgroup.com**. Outside of the U.S., please contact: International Sales (317) 428-3341 or **international@pearsontechgroup.com**.

WRITE TO US

New Riders Publishing
800 East 96th Street, 3rd floor
Indianapolis, IN 46240

CALL US

Toll-free (800) 571-5840. Ask for New Riders.
If outside U.S. (317) 428-3000. Ask for New Riders.

FAX US

(317) 428-3280

New Riders

  ## CUSTOM WELCOME SCREEN

That super-handy screen that you see when Dreamweaver starts (unless you've disabled it) can be even more useful. In the main program configuration, look for welcome.dwt inside Dreamweaver MX 2004\Configuration\Content\Welcome\. There is a copy of this file in your user's configuration, too, but customizing it won't do you any good. This is the one instance that I know of where you must make changes to the main configuration on a multi-user operating system. Consider the file in your user's configuration a backup if you happen to make a mistake while changing the one in the main configuration. You can change welcome.dwt all you like, but I suggest you look at Code view when doing so to be sure you don't break any of the functionality for things such as the Most Recent Files list. You'll also find two CSS files in the same location as welcome.dwt. If you're a Windows user, stylesWin.css is the file you can modify. Macintosh users can make changes to stylesMac.css.

Even though it has the .dwt file extension and uses Dreamweaver template syntax, it doesn't control any HTML files in the configuration at the time you save the file. On startup, the welcome.dwt file is used to produce welcome.htm found in your user's configuration. You may want to look at welcome.htm for examples of how to link to specific files on your computer if that is part of your customization needs.

INDEX

www.informit.com

YOUR GUIDE TO IT REFERENCE

New Riders has partnered with **InformIT.com** to bring technical information to your desktop. Drawing from New Riders authors and reviewers to provide additional information on topics of interest to you, **InformIT.com** provides free, in-depth information you won't find anywhere else.

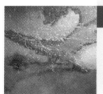

Articles

Keep your edge with thousands of free articles, in-depth features, interviews, and IT reference recommendations— all written by experts you know and trust.

Online Books

Answers in an instant from **InformIT Online Books'** 600+ fully searchable online books.

POWERED BY

Catalog

Review online sample chapters, author biographies, and customer rankings, and choose exactly the right book from a selection of over 5,000 titles.

ww.newriders.com

VISIT OUR WEB SITE

WWW.NEWRIDERS.COM

On our Web site you'll find information about our other books, authors, tables of contents, indexes, and book errata. You will also find information about book registration and how to purchase our books.

EMAIL US

Contact us at this address: **nrfeedback@newriders.com**

- If you have comments or questions about this book
- To report errors that you have found in this book
- If you have a book proposal to submit or are interested in writing for New Riders
- If you would like to have an author kit sent to you
- If you are an expert in a computer topic or technology and are interested in being a technical editor who reviews manuscripts for technical accuracy

- To find a distributor in your area, please contact our international department at this address: **nrmedia@newriders.com**

- For instructors from educational institutions who want to preview New Riders books for classroom use. Email should include your name, title, school, department, address, phone number, office days/hours, text in use, and enrollment, along with your request for desk/examination copies and/or additional information.
- For members of the media who are interested in reviewing copies of New Riders books. Send your name, mailing address, and email address, along with the name of the publication or Web site you work for.

BULK PURCHASES/CORPORATE SALES

The publisher offers discounts on this book when ordered in quantity for bulk purchases and special sales. For sales within the U.S., please contact: Corporate and Government Sales (800) 382-3419 or **corpsales@pearsontechgroup.com**. Outside of the U.S., please contact: International Sales (317) 428-3341 or **international@pearsontechgroup.com**.

WRITE TO US

New Riders Publishing
800 East 96th Street, 3rd floor
Indianapolis, IN 46240

CALL US

Toll-free (800) 571-5840. Ask for New Riders.
If outside U.S. (317) 428-3000. Ask for New Riders.

FAX US

(317) 428-3280

Voices
that Matter ™

OUR AUTHORS

PRESS ROOM

| :::: web development | :::: design | :::: photoshop | :::: new media | :::: 3-D | :::: server te |

You already know that New Riders brings you the **Voices That Matter**. But what does that mean? It means that New Riders brings you the Voices that challenge your assumptions, take your talents to the next level, or simply help you better understand the complex technical world we're all navigating.

EDUCATORS

ABOUT US

CONTACT US

Visit **www.newriders.com** to find:

- ▸ *Discounts* on specific book purchases
- ▸ Never before published chapters
- ▸ Sample chapters and excerpts
- ▸ Author bios and interviews
- ▸ Contests and enter-to-wins
- ▸ Up-to-date industry event information
- ▸ Book reviews
- ▸ Special offers from our friends and partners
- ▸ Info on how to join our User Group program
  Ways to have your Voice heard

New
Riders

WWW.NEWRIDERS.COM